Grand Luxe

A *Glamorous* FIRST GLIMPSE of EUROPE

Grand Luxe

The Transatlantic Style

John Malcolm Brinnin and

Kenneth Gaulin

HENRY HOLT AND COMPANY · NEW YORK

For Michael C. J. Putnam

and for Frank E. Taylor

Europe by Way of "The Rock."
(Half title illustration) A *frisson* of antic-
ipation mobilizes the privileged occupants
of a verandah suite *di lusso* aboard Italy's
Rex as the ship sails past Gibraltar and
into the blue waters of the Mediterranean.

Poster Art.
(Frontispiece) Imposing and indomitable,
Aquitania arrives in New York, her four-
funneled magnificence standing in relief
before the gilded *nomen* of her sponsor. At
45,647 tons, a larger sister to *Lusitania*
and *Mauretania*, she was much the more
opulent and luxurious.

Copyright © 1988 by John Malcolm Brinnin and Kenneth Gaulin
All rights reserved, including the right to reproduce
this book or portions thereof in any form.
Published by Henry Holt and Company, Inc.,
115 West 18th Street, New York, New York 10011.
Published in Canada by Fitzhenry & Whiteside Limited,
195 Allstate Parkway, Markham, Ontario L3R 4T8.

Library of Congress Cataloging-in-Publication Data
Brinnin, John Malcolm, 1916–
Grand luxe.
Includes index.
1. Ocean Liners.   I. Gaulin, Kenneth.   II. Title.
VM381.B699   1988   623.8'2432   87-37656
ISBN 0-8050-0899-3

First Edition

Designed by Katy Homans with Jody Hanson
Printed in Italy
10 9 8 7 6 5 4 3 2 1

ISBN 0-8050-0899-3

Acknowledgments

The Steamer Cap.
Once de rigueur, the steamer cap continued to distinguish the frequent ocean traveler until well into the fifties. It then joined the inverness, plus fours, and the Norfolk jacket in the discarded wardrobe of seagoing.

For major assistance in assembling the graphic materials, the authors thank (CANADA) David Jones, CP Rail; (ENGLAND) Capt. Doug Ridley, Ronald Warwick, Cunard Line; Peter Boyd-Smith; Liverpool University Archives; Chris Maygar; Mewès & Davis, Archs.; D. F. Payne, Darius & Nordon Art Co.; Judith Dagworthy, Dr. Pat Kelvin, Savoy Hotel; (FRANCE) René Bouvard; Albert Brenet; Bibl. de la Marine; François Capiomont; Susan Day, Inst. Français d'Architecture; Musée des Arts Décoratifs; Jean de Moüy, Patou; Domenique Clemenceau, Laure de Gramont, Louis Vuitton; (GERMANY) Andrea Pohl, Karl Th. Walterspiel, Atlantic Kempinsky Hotel; Dr. Jörgan Bracker, Mus. für Hamburgische Geschichte; Dr. Detlev Elmers, Arnold Kludas, Deutsches Schiffahrtsmuseum; Dr. Peter Hahn; Rolf Finck, Eva Gjersvik, Erika Lisson, Dirk Penner, H. Rickmann, Gerhard Simonsen, Hapag-Lloyd; (ITALY) Dr. Paolo Valenti, Aldebaron Soc.; *Domus*; Martha Baldini; Rossana Bossaglia; Prof. G. Chigiotti; Silvana Brondi, Francesco Cattaneo, CIGA Hotels; Flavio Costantini; Mauro Cozzi; Dr. T. Favaretto, Lloyd-Triestino; Elizabetta Feliziani; Maria Flora Giubelei; Louisa Chiodarolli, Annamaria Ghiazza, "Italia"; Dr. Allessandro Lombardo, Ansaldo; Museo Tech. di Milano; Dr. Donato Riccesi; Allessandra Verdona; (UNITED STATES) Harvey Ardman; Frank O. Braynard; Amer. Soc. of Illustrators; Cooper-Hewitt Library; Susan Alpert, Alice Marshall, Ralph Bahna, Cunard Line; Charles Flynn; The Atlantic Companies; Mark Goldberg; William A. Guthrie; Ted Hindmarsh; John Hollis; Carl House; Gay Jacobson; Edward Kamuda, *Titanic* Hist. Soc.; The Forbes Coll.; Trude Lash; Peter Lauritzen; Paul Richards Lemma; Ken Marschall; Norman McGrath; Mus. of the City of N.Y.; William H. Miller; Nat. Geo. Soc.; Bruce Newman, Newel Art Galleries; Pan Am. World Airways; Peabody Museum; Barbara Post; James Finley, R.I. Sch. of Des. Library; Hugh Stockmeyer; Wood Sutton; Time Life, Inc.; Frank Trumbour; Olav Wahlund; Mark D. Warren; Stephen Greengard, Pamela Johnson, and Mitchell Wolfson, Jr., The Wolfson Initiative.

For acts of kindness and patience in response to our questions, we thank Lillian Berliewsky; M. Grant Boyd; Nina Bremer; Clementine Brown; David Campbell, Hotel Ritz, Paris; M. & Mme. Michel Capiomont; Enza Cirrincione, CIGA Hotels, N.Y.; Marie Cosindas; Alberto Cosulich; Paolo U. Cosulich; Prof. John Davies; Desmond Elliott; Prof. Michael Fink; Véronique Forgeot, Hôtel de Crillon, Paris; William Fraiberg; Mr. & Mrs. Joseph E. Gaulin; Rose Gilford; Victor Glasstone; Peter Haack; Daniel Jones; Mr. & Mrs. Richard Jones; Kay Kuhn; Kenneth Lough; M. & Mme. A. Mahuzier; Brigitte Mahuzier; Rollie McKenna; Madeda Mina, Marchésa di Sospiro; Jan Morris; Charles Pierce; Mr. & Mrs. Pietro Pucci; Holly Poindexter; Deborah Richardson; Nancy Roelker; Richard Schneider; The Hon. Richard Shepherd, M.P.; Arnold Silverman; Jana Slapin, The Leading Hotels of the World; Robert Stanton; Alice Stein; Anna Lowell Tomlinson; *Vogue*, London; David Wolkowsky; and Russell Young.

Contents

S. S. LEVIATHAN

WORLD'S LARGEST SHIP

Introduction

At Home Abroad.
The sartorially impeccable chap above—
drawn by Leslie Saalburg, premier delin-
eator of men's fashions in the 1930s—
carries his polo coat and attaché case
down a rubber-treaded gangplank onto a
North River pier. Saalburg's accurate detailing of background suggests our traveler
is disembarking from either *Bremen* or
Europa of Norddeutscher Lloyd. *(Facing
page)* An advertisement of 1924 made it
clear that to cross on one of Cunard Line's
great postwar trio—*Aquitania, Berengaria,
Mauretania*—was in no way to travel
"light."

Barely a century old, yet already afloat in the distant past, the luxury liner of legend was made possible by two factors of nuts-and-bolts practicality. First, a shift in structural dimensions allowing as much shipboard space for glass-domed saloons and winter gardens as for bunkers and boilers. Second, an encouraging record of safety at sea that caused embarking passengers to show as much interest in comforts and novel facilities that might beguile them as in the clumsy jackets and greasy lifeboats that might save them.

At the magic moment when, late in the nineteenth century, these conditions were met, interior designers with a flair for the sumptuous and eclectic were ready to enter the business of sea travel. Passenger transportation would soon become the most glamorous maritime enterprise since the empire-building British East India Company of 1600 and the Hudson's Bay Company of 1670. Within a mere twenty years from the day when some anonymous designer rolled out bolts of watered silk, toyed with the placement of mirrors and emblematic statuary, then applied gilt to a lily wrought of iron, his commercial importance to steamship operators was already on the way to becoming greater than that of shipwright and engineer combined.

The following chapters record the names of those who gave passenger ships identities akin to world-famous personalities, and document their individual contributions to the nebulous but endlessly evocative reflection of social deportment and *haut-monde* preference here called "the transatlantic style." Aesthetically speaking, that style is a composite of period-piece echoes and short-lived notions of the contemporary—from the spacious opulence decreed by disciples of Beaux Arts in the nineteenth century to the first shy glimmerings of high tech in the third decade of the twentieth. It is also an index to the social privileges and restrictions of a time when crossing the Atlantic was not a few hours of supersonic expediency but a week or more of long-established custom and protocol among "persons"—as Oscar Wilde's Lady Bracknell or the Marx Brothers' Margaret Dumont might say—"of one's own class and kind."

Luxury at sea or, for that matter, even on water, has a peculiarly brief and intermittent history. The Bible is no help at all in determining the class system on Noah's Ark; and it says nothing about the way in which its human complement might have maintained a certain distance from the rampant informality of its coupled and no doubt coupling beasts. In literature, luxury afloat begins with Cleopatra's barge. And if we are to take Shakespeare's word for it:

Shore to Ship and Vice Versa.
In settings of *alta borghese* splendor like
the dining room above, the Grand Hotel
Colombia offered an introduction to life at
sea for travelers outward bound and a
reprise of floating-palace ambience for
those just disembarked. Built in response
to expanding passenger traffic on routes
into the Atlantic and situated mere minutes from Genoa's *stazione marittima*, the
Colombia opened its doors in 1929 but had
precedents as far back as Hamburg's Hotel
Atlantic of 1909 and Liverpool's Adelphi of
1914—each of which reflected "the steamship style" or *le stile paquebot* many years
before these terms had come into currency.
(*CIGA Hotels, Milan*)

La Scala at Sea.
(*Left*) With respects due in equal measure
to Giovanni Piranesi, Hugh Ferriss, and
Busby Berkeley, the Italian Line offered
this impression, in 1934, of the theatrical
splendor awaiting Southern Route travelers
aboard its new flagship and Blue Riband
holder, *Rex*.

The barge she sat in, like a burnished throne,

Burned on the water; the poop was beaten gold,

Purple the sails, and so perfumed, that

The winds were love-sick with them; the oars were silver,

Which to the tune of flutes kept stroke . . .

that early example of royal conveyance was every bit as sumptuous as the floating villas and waterborne gardens of Caligula's galleys before those grotesque structures came to rest, all of a piece, in the oozy depths of Lake Nemi.

Still, Cleopatra's vessel was strictly a riverboat, a kind of showboat; and Caligula's galleys, spidering around a little freshwater lake, went nowhere. On the broad ocean, travel in cushioned ease within ornamented space was not available at any price until the fifteenth century. Then, high-pooped Spanish caravels and galleons set in motion a series of changes that would, first, remove the "quality" from the aft ends of these many-masted ships into coffin-like enclosures in their still-dismal depths and, eventually, put affluent passengers in cabins and social rooms placed even higher than the once sacrosanct quarters of the captain himself.

Before these developments had quite run their course, provincial America was the unlikely proving ground for some of the first manifestations of supererogatory luxury. This phenomenon was "Steamboat Gothic"—a term referring to the look of river craft plying the Mississippi and the Hudson contemporaneous with coastal steamers of a similar type running from New Orleans to Savannah, Cape May to Newport, New York to Stonington and Fall River. Their hulls all but invisible, these many-tiered wedding cakes, all superstructure, showed off a brand of homegrown elegance soon to become international—vast oval galleries for evening promenades; lounges of scarlet plush, outlined in gilt, off which were ranged cubbies upholstered as heavily as opera boxes; dining rooms reflecting the candlelight of sconces and crystal chandeliers; cabins as cozy as the insides of carpetbags.

In comfort and appointment far ahead of the British and American paddle-wheelers, which, from 1840 onward, rolled and racketed from New York and Boston to Liverpool, these low-draft and top-heavy steamers offered their own kind of glamour, along with a standard of white-jacketed service otherwise encountered only in the plantation houses of the South. But when their virtues were translated into the idiom of the first true luxury liners—all of them from Germany—only those aspects that might be described as bordello baroque were much in evidence. Consequently, the American contribution to the first phase of *Raumkunst an Bord*—as the Germans called ship decoration—was not so much a reminder of antebellum graciousness as of the hearty vulgarity of the *maisons de tolérance* of the Louisiana Purchase.

However unexpected its source, that first touch of luxury opened the way to a pageant on the North Atlantic lasting for more than eighty years. Generation to generation, an international flotilla renewed itself with a sense of grandeur broad enough to launch seagoing versions of castles on the Rhine, châteaus on the Loire, stately homes from Sussex and Surrey, along with the megalithic villas of the Risorgimento and the marble cottages of Newport.

Deck Life.
Latter-day images depicting activity at sea as taking place in bikinis and suntan oil tend to obscure the fact that outdoor swimming pools were rare on transatlantic liners until late in the century. Bundled in steamer robes, passengers would be grateful for the two or three days of a crossing when ocean winds on uncovered decks were tolerable. Here, with uncommon realism, painter Carl Bergen pictures fully clothed outdoor activity on Norddeutscher Lloyd's 32,000-ton *Columbus* in 1924. *(Arnold Kludas, Deutsches Schiffahrtsmuseum, Bremerhaven)*

All of them afloat at the same time, ocean liners in the images of their origins continued to sail like vigorous revenants of an age unaware that its term was up. A few of them were still going strong when, one day in 1958, the first jet passenger plane, streaking from Idlewild to Croydon in six hours, sent them circling into exile, oblivion, or careers of expensive nullity which, for a little while, could do no more than parody "the way it was."

Our subject is a phase of maritime history synonymous with high life—fifty years of extravagance and *folie de grandeur* on the North Atlantic's arc of sea-lanes known as the Great Circle. Since that life took place in ever changing settings, these pages also represent a first attempt to name and relate developments in marine architecture and interior decoration that produced the luxury liners and ocean greyhounds of the late nineteenth century and the floating palaces and oil-fired "cathedrals of steel" of the twentieth.

Our story begins with business-as-usual in the seawise city of Bremen. It ends as a romantic legend sustained by nostalgia and exploited by purveyors of luxury goods in their search for images of fashion *à la mode* and metaphors for chic. Into whatever byways our narrative leads, its burden is simple: a once modest expectation of comfort and safety at sea turns, almost overnight, into a demand for sumptuousness and theatrical ambience never curbed or sated until, on a February morning in 1942, the glittering pavilions of the *Normandie* are toppled into the mud of the Hudson River.

The myth of transatlantica is a creation of our own times. Often recalled like some aspect of ancient history, it is based on sober technological facts and certified by astonishing artifacts. An idea of romance, as well as a well-kept chronicle of sea travel, transatlantica calls for documentation that excludes neither its reality nor its hyperbole.

With this in mind, our aim has been to make *Grand Luxe* a museum-between-covers where visible evidence, labeled and placed in sequence, re-creates one of the briefest and merriest moments of cultural archaeology. If our efforts ratify the claims of those who regard the ocean liner as the ultimate embodiment of a way of life governed by style and conducted with grace, we will have satisfied their fantasies, and confirmed our own.

John Malcolm Brinnin
Kenneth Gaulin

CLAUS BERGEN
AN BORD D. "COLUMBUS"
APRIL-MAI 1924

PART ONE

The German Invention: *Luxus* at Sea

Speisesaal.
The meringue baroque of Johannes Poppe's
dining room on the *Kaiser Wilhelm II*
reached upward through three decks suffused in the radiance of a skylight dome of
many-colored glass. The opportunity to
dine in a well of cathedral light removed
forever the mess-hall institutionalism of
mealtime at sea and encouraged passengers to dress with a formality appropriate to the sacerdotal atmosphere. *(Hapag-
Lloyd Archive, Bremen)*

Available to those accustomed to it—as well as to those with the means to buy it—luxury as a mode of travel was only the first of many surprising German contributions to the steamship era. But the idea of making an ocean crossing a socially gratifying experience was not without its precedents: America's Collins Line of the middle nineteenth century had loaded its speedy hell-bent-for-leather liners with all the embellishments of riverboat baroque; and Great Britain's innovative *Oceanic* of 1870 had ended the custom of confining privileged passengers to nether regions of ships affording daylight only in porthole glimpses or in hazardous huddlings amid the winch-and-hawser clutter of open decks. Extending the full breadth of the ship, the *Oceanic*'s grand saloon, lighted by circular bull's-eyes that looked onto the sea, had coal-burning fireplaces and marble mantels at each end. In her dining room, the great new thing was the introduction of separate armchairs, obviating the need to get up from a settee "of undefined capacity," serviette in hand, for latecomers, and instilling confidence that, in a moment of dreadful urgency, quick exit was possible. After dinner, when it was time for the segregation of the sexes, ladies could retire to a little boudoir encased in brocades and hung with mirrors; gentlemen could repair to a Smoking Room that was "quite a narcotic paradise" with windows and doors open to sea and sky, or closed to both. At long last, a man and his cigar did not have to go behind the barn.

Yet these conveniences were mere prelude to a phase of comfort unknown on the Atlantic when German ships, beginning with those from Bremen under the aegis of architect-designer Johannes Georg Poppe, began to sail off like fully equipped villas and town houses detached from the lots on which they stood. This imitative phase of German *Luxus* threatened to perpetuate itself in ever larger versions of prevailing domestic architecture until the very end of the century. Then its dependence upon the overstuffed and overwrought began to be modified by the influence of styles ranging from Viennese Secessionism to Italian Liberty, or Floreale, and the several continental manifestations of Art Nouveau. This intrusion, gingerly welcomed, if not embraced, by Poppe and his disciples, became a turning point in the fortunes of Norddeutscher Lloyd and, as it turned out, guaranteed that company's aesthetic preeminence for a generation.

In Hamburg, meanwhile, under the close collaboration of chief executive Albert Ballin and his designer-architect, Charles Mewès, the ships of Hamburg-Amerika continued to exhibit artifacts and replicas from the storehouse of European history on a scale without precedent. Tit for tat, the two Hanseatic pioneers remained locked in creative rivalry until World War I dropped a curtain on tradition and experiment alike.

NORDDEUTSCHER LLOYD, *ARCHITEKT* POPPE, AND *BREMISCHES BAROCK*

Der Meister.
Johannes Georg Poppe, who made tradition seem like novelty by the simple expedient of taking centuries of it to sea intact. His villas, town houses, and civic buildings were the pride of Bremen before he turned his lavish hand to ships.

    Preparing himself for a career as an architect and interior decorator, Poppe had traveled extensively in France and Italy. His sketchbooks reveal a dutiful interest in Pompeiian wall paintings but a distinct preference for the domestic baroque—like this corner *(left)* of the principal *salone* of Palazzo Barbaro in Venice—the levitating forms and swirling patterns of which he would carry home to Bremen and, over a period of twenty-five years, re-create in the swaying saloons of a long succession of Norddeutscher Lloyd steamers. *(Courtesy of Peter Lauritzen)*

Almost seventy years after transatlantic travel had become a schedule-keeping operation, steamers were distinguished only by their speed and size, and by the temperaments of their commanding officers. Luxury had not yet become a selling point, simply because—beyond the promise of an organ to accompany hymn-singing, or gas lighting that would extend the customary ten-o'clock curfew—it was nonexistent. Touches of comfort, on the other hand, were featured in company advertisements—"Turkey" carpets on cabin floors, swivel chairs at dining tables, systems of bells for the summoning of stewards. If no mention was made of the fact that ablutions were limited to those made with water poured from a jug into a bowl, or that other sanitary functions were dependent upon *pots de chambre* emptied, leeward, every morning, few passengers expected that ships would offer anything more in the way of personal hygiene than what they were used to at home. Deck life, as represented in illustrations of handsome women wearing blouses with leg-o'-mutton sleeves and jaunty boaters, was deceptive. A walk on deck was apt to be taken only in order to escape for a few minutes the human effluvia of unventilated saloons and the *olla podrida* of which the famous and pervasive "ship's smell" was composed. The letters and journals of generations of passengers attest to the fact that almost any voyage on the North Atlantic was something between horror unalleviated and a grim test of endurance. All that was about to undergo change. Affluent travelers would no longer, at sea, put up with anything less than what they took as their due on land, including the space and attention that money could buy and, in some cases, the airs it allowed them to put on.

When the field was open to any designer capable of bringing the trappings of domestic luxury to ships' interiors, one of the first to accept the task was the German architect Johannes Poppe.

Classically trained, and philosophically in accord with those Beaux Arts ideals embraced by Europe's expanding middle class, Poppe was already a public figure. As the man responsible for a number of Bremen's exemplary civic buildings and many of its most elaborate residences, he had made a mark in his hometown that would lead to his becoming its official architect.

Within the first few years of his employment as a maritime designer, Poppe made contributions so confidently grand and so unexpected by the workaday shipping world that his bravado was recognized as "the momentous turning point in the history of interior decoration of ships." Among the pocket-sized luxury liners he produced in the 1880s was the *Lahn* (one of a series named after German rivers), each of them a seaborne gesture toward hyperbole that started a race for ornamentation and eye-catching novelty that would last for more than sixty years.

Forerunner.
Norddeutscher Lloyd's single-screw, 5,681-ton *Lahn*, showing auxiliary sail, makes way through scrappy seas in this engraving dating from 1887, the year of her maiden voyage from Bremen to New York.

Despite austere externals, the *Lahn* carried within her hull and modest super-structure Johannes Poppe's first major con-tribution to seagoing *Luxus* and so became the prototype of the luxury liner with "artistic forms" that were "the glittering robe . . . made to cover enforced exigen-cies."

The *Lahn*'s jewel-box velvets and gilded cornices were audacious mostly because they signaled the transference of familiar land-based touches of elegance to the unfamiliar setting of a ship at sea. But the truly original thing about the *Lahn* and her sister ships was an idea—a conviction that it was time to change ocean crossings from ordeals to be endured into pleasures to be savored. Opulence was about to replace comfort as a selling point, luxury about to discount security and punctuality. Stem to stern, the *Lahn* reflected the taste of a period of growing affluence when the imitation of French and Italian artifacts of the Renaissance combined to produce in *Strasse* and *Platz* a peculiarly native amalgamation of styles that would become known as *"Bremisches Barock."*

What Poppe did with the *Lahn* was what every other maritime designer for the next forty years would do: take the drawing rooms of burghers, or the reading rooms of St. James's gentlemen's clubs, disguise the means by which they were fitted into the contours of limited shipboard space, and send them to sea intact.

Before he came to be inescapably associated with *Raumkunst an Bord*, Poppe had spent a leisurely *Wanderjahr* in France and Italy. But whatever his own developing interests may have been, there is ample evidence that he could not escape the overpowering hold on European architecture that the École des Beaux Arts of Paris exerted. Back home in Bremen by 1863, his notebooks filled with delicate sketches of rooftops of the boulevards of Baron Haussmann and Roman frescoes from Pompeii, he began practice with a sort of eclectic

conservatism as apparent in his monumental civic buildings as in the town houses and villas he designed for the mercantile elite. Among the expanding enterprises of his native city was the steamship company Norddeutscher Lloyd, then largely a carrier of emigrants to the New World in competition with its Hanseatic neighbor, Hamburg-Amerika. But the business image of both companies as purveyors of mass transit for the dispossessed of Mittel-Europa was about to undergo a profound change. Assured of continuing profit from the emigrant trade, the directors of both firms turned their attention to speed, then to amenities, and soon to conspicuous overlays of luxury. At once, German ships took precedence over those of other nations even while they were themselves engaged in a rivalry based on gilded stairwells, rotundas of stained glass, *Rauchzimmern* (smoking rooms) of baronial proportions, and before long, the favor and imprimatur of the royal family.

In the last of these, Norddeutscher Lloyd achieved a public relations coup by winning endorsements that gave its prestige a boost maintained for more than a decade. The Hohenzollerns allowed the ships of Bremen to bear their royal names, christened them in widely publicized launching ceremonies, and even traveled in them.

These imperial commendations were not lost on the overseas clientele most likely to fill the line's First Class accommodations. This was a new breed of Americans who were cultured, rich, or both, hungry for the experience of Europe that was essential to social status, or for whom the "grand tour" had become an entitlement of privilege as routinely taken for granted as an Ivy League education. Unlike their British counterparts who

Kaiser Wilhelm der Grosse.
Paired funnels fore and aft—characteristic
of German liners until 1909—opened up
midships space for broad, high public
rooms, particularly those lighted by glass
domes. This cutaway view also indicates
the vast and disproportionate amount of
cubic space which, as late as 1897, was
allotted to storage and the housing of
mechanisms.

Comparisons.
(Facing page) Left to right, the first
Bremen, 2,551 tons (1857); the
Kronprinzessin Cecilie, 19,360 tons (1907);
and the *Lahn*, 5,681 tons (1887). *(Hapag-
Lloyd Archive, Bremen)*

looked upon "abroad" as a nebulous region of unsuitable customs and unsettling license and who regarded travel as a penitential term spent in "roughing it," these Americans wanted to go in ease and style; and Norddeutscher Lloyd was there to provide both.

In the wide swaths of *putti*, grilles of wrought iron, and tufted leather cut by Johannes Poppe, that company led the way in ship decoration for three decades—years in which the master's preferences were ineffectively challenged by everything from the revelations of Art Nouveau put on display in the van der Velde rooms of Dresden in 1896 to the instant classics of interior design being produced by the school of Charles Rennie Mackintosh in Glasgow. In a time of rapid changes in advanced taste, Poppe's settled notions of *Luxus* continued to be part of the company's offerings; and the weight of his presence was central to its determination to set the standard of *Erste Klasse* on the ocean.

Nevertheless, there was a growing feeling on the part of some of Norddeutscher Lloyd's executives that "Poppe's baroque"—to which by now every last carpenter, ironworker, and bricklayer in Bremen had contributed his mite—had reached its zenith in a "witches' sabbath of ornament and curlicues, of cartouches and figures, of grilles and sills." It might be wise, they thought, to give younger designers an opportunity to show at sea those revisions of established ideas of domestic decor they had already succeeded in making popular on land.

For all that, Poppe had no reason to feel threatened. His recent completion of Bremen's City Library and its gracefully massive Cotton Exchange had brought him renewed acclaim; and the delicacy of his designs for the *Damensalon* aboard the new *Kaiser Wilhelm der Grosse* was considered a triumph. His local preeminence was secure.

ATELIER BOLLHAGEN BREMEN

Boarding House Reach.
The refectory table, with chairs designed
to swivel—as much for hasty retreats in
rough weather as for normal ease in sitting
down or getting up—was a standard
feature of ships' restaurants until early in
the twentieth century. When it was replaced by tables seating two to eight, the
tradition of the groaning board it represented was continued in the custom of
elaborate buffets or smorgasbords, some
with monumental sculptures of pastry or
ice, and huge cornucopias of fruit, situated
so as to confront entering diners with
theatrical previews of the feast in store.
(Mark Goldberg Collection)

The Enchantment of Travel.
(Right) Lost in dreams of far-off places,
the well-turned-out ladies on the deck of a
Norddeutscher Lloyd steamer are apparently unaware that their lovely frocks are
about to be ruined in a cloud of smuts from
the passing Kaiser Wilhelm der Grosse.
(Hapag-Lloyd Archive, Bremen)

Damensalon.
While the leathery shipboard smoking room was out of bounds for ladies, gentlemen were accepted, if not welcomed, in delicately ornate retreats for women passengers that remained a feature of ocean liners almost until World War I. The intimate salon pictured at right, minus *putti* and *purdah*, was installed in Norddeutscher Lloyd's *Kaiser Wilhelm der Grosse* of 1897.

Full Speed Ahead.
In tune with the spirit of ominous times,
painters and other illustrators tended to
make German liners of the early century
seem aggressive, fearsome, and in a hurry.
Even the *Kronprinzessin Cecilie*—as de-
mure in style and manner as her namesake—is here subject to a kind of
treatment by which the simple act of
sailing away is interpreted as bearing
down. *(Hapag-Lloyd Archive, Bremen)*

Vienna Café.
The *Kronprinzessin Cecilie*'s à la carte restaurant appealed to those travelers seeking more intimacy than the grandiose, triple-tiered *speisesaal* of the ordinary *Erste Klasse* could provide. Besides exclusivity, it offered elegantly molded paneling, space-enhancing mirrors—including an arched "window" with reflecting panes—and an airy, domed ceiling.

On the night of July 31, 1914, word came to the patrons of the Café—some of whom were expecting to disembark at Plymouth for Scotland and the grouse season, others to leave the ship at Bremerhaven for the fashionable spas of the Rhineland—that they had just turned 180 degrees and were headed back to neutral American waters and, as it developed, disembarkation into the fringe-on-top launches of Bar Harbor's Frenchman Bay. *(Ted and Joan Hindmarsh Collection)*

Yet in the first decade of the century, parochial reputations were everywhere being undermined by forces indifferent to boundaries. Neither smug nor open-minded, caught in swift currents of transition, Poppe was something of an enigma to his associates. "He remained standing at the gate of the ultra modern," said one of them, "not because he could not have entered, but evidently because he did not want to."

In any case, celebrated by his employers as *der Meister*, but nevertheless kept on tether, Poppe had to witness the rise of Jugendstil (the German equivalent of the revisionist or Secessionist art movements cropping up everywhere on the Continent) and to acquiesce in the humiliation of having to work side by side with the Young Turks of a new dispensation.

The penultimate ship to come from the drawing boards of Bremen before World War I, the *Kronprinzessin Cecilie* was the last of the line in which the grand old man would play a hand—even though its reach was limited by a new turn toward the simple and reductive. Assigned to do the *Kronprinzessin*'s public rooms, Poppe disguised his distrust of Jugendstil by adopting some of its modest traceries to purposes of his own. The result was a ship, conceived in the grand manner, which nevertheless gave the appearance of something fresh from the *Kunst und Handwerk* ateliers of Berlin and the entrepôts of cosmopolitan influences they had come to be.

Schnelldampfer
„Kronprinzessin Cecilie“.

Speisesaal I. Klasse
mit der neuen Anordnung der Tische.

Entwurf
von Joh. G. Poppe, Bremen.

Express Steamer
"Kronprinzessin Cecilie".

I. Class Saloon,
showing the new arrangement of the tables

Designed
by Joh. G. Poppe, Bremen.

Reprise.

(Left) Less baroque and considerably more formal than his dining room on the *Kaiser Wilhelm II*, Johannes Poppe's contribution to the *Kronprinzessin Cecilie* indicates his acceptance of the lighter touch of his young contemporaries without loss of his own signature. With this room, Poppe came to the end of a career which, nearly twenty-five years earlier, was responsible for the expansive elegance and fantasy of luxury on voyages once considered trials of endurance, or passages of the soul akin to purgatory.

(Above) Pillars and a skylight dome— the spacious formality of *Kronprinzessin Cecilie*'s Smoking Room. *(Both pictures from the Ted and Joan Hindmarsh Collection)*

A reincarnation of the seagoing grandeur Poppe had been himself the first to introduce, the *Kronprinzessin Cecilie* was, all to his credit, the last German liner to honor the gravity of tradition without denying the appeal of the new.

And yet, for all of her distinction as the flagship of Norddeutscher Lloyd's golden age, history would see to it that she would be remembered less as a maritime masterpiece than as the heroine of a dramatic wartime cause célèbre. When she sailed out of New York in July 1914, the *Kronprinzessin* was dubbed "the treasure ship"—a reference to the fact that she was carrying fourteen million dollars' worth of gold and silver bullion dispatched by the Guaranty Trust and National Trust companies for settlements of American accounts abroad. Caught by the outbreak of war when she was two-thirds of the way across the Atlantic, she was ordered, in a coded wireless message from Berlin, at once to seek haven in the United States. Abruptly reversing course, she raced through fog in which lurked squadrons of British cruisers well informed of her whereabouts. Then, with an appropriateness almost too good to be true, she was piloted into the waters of Bar Harbor's Frenchman Bay by one of her yachtsman passengers familiar with each of its coves and juts of granite. Haven, however, was no guarantee of freedom.

Perfectly timed to hit the very height of the season, the *Kronprinzessin*'s escapade allowed her captain and officers to join Bar Harbor's social rounds and her musically inclined crew to give band concerts on the village green. But as it turned out, she had also made a dash toward confiscation and a pillar-to-post existence as an American hostage of war. Recommissioned as a troopship, she was dismantled inside and camouflaged without. Her grand saloon became a doughboys' dormitory; and her vast and airy *Speisesaal*—the last gift of Johannes Poppe to the era he had initiated—was reduced to a mess hall and scullery.

Historically speaking, Poppe's career, from Beaux Arts to his own version of Art Nouveau, identifies him as the first designer of steamship interiors to stand foursquare as a reference and a source. His professional background was little different from that of any other aspiring young architect, with one exception—the intriguing possibility that his original breakthrough from comfort to unabashed luxury in ocean carriers was influenced not only by the *piani nobili* of Renaissance *palazzi* but by the homegrown American decor of steamboats plying the Mississippi. This connection has been suggested by Otto Hover, the most eminent contemporary German historian of naval architecture, and given further weight by the documentation of Poppe's intimate contact with a client, Otto Frerichs, a cotton broker who had for years traveled on these American boats in the course of his business pursuits. When, in 1880, Frerichs and his French wife returned to Bremen from New Orleans, they commissioned Poppe to build them a house that would combine the architect's own classicism with what they remembered of the carved mahogany, glowing plush, and general theatricality of the American style. The result, on land, was the Villa Frerichs am Osterdeich and, at sea, ocean liners in which Medicean pretensions were modified by the cheerier elegance of Dixie.

LUXUS REDEFINED —
S. S. GEORGE WASHINGTON

Homeward Bound.
Her ocher stacks glowing through North River overcast, the 25,570-ton *George Washington* of 1908 backs out of her Hoboken berth and sets a course for Bremerhaven. A conservative appearance gives no hint of the extraordinary interiors that make her noteworthy in the annals of the steamship era. *(Deutsches Schiffahrtsmuseum, Bremerhaven)*

"A Merry Chat on the Boat Deck."
The publicist's caption omits the fact that this photograph could have been made only when the *George Washington* was in port where the hats of these lady passengers, or models pretending to be, were not at the mercy of ocean breezes.
　　Posed or not, this promotional photo was made immediately aft of the ship's bridge and depicts, not only the millinery mode of the moment, but also Norddeutscher Lloyd's predilection in those years for a dark, reddish-brown paint color on the superstructures of its ships. *(Hapag-Lloyd Archive, Bremen)*

Spooling lines and whiplash curlicues, sprays, sprigs, and floriated abstractions—the iconography of Art Nouveau had by 1900 made its brief but worldwide impression and begun to fade back into the curious period of ersatz medievalism in mid-Victorian England from which it derived. By that same year, an equally fleeting moment of decorative history—the Chippendale-Georgian of late American colonialism—had become little more than a reference-book entry, perhaps illustrated with tinted views of Mount Vernon. The possibility that these unrelated phases of design might be joined was remote, or about as likely as a vision of George Washington clothed in an Aubrey Beardsley fig leaf or, by the same token, Beardsley turned out in the full fig of the general. But so they were, on the decks of the *George Washington*, a liner so far removed from the accepted taste of her time as to represent, and remain, one of the happier sports of maritime history.

　　Incongruous at first thought, this combination was not made without calculation. As Hamburg-Amerika continued to attract a larger portion of the American trade, Norddeutscher Lloyd was keen to lure away its customers—especially those who were not recent emigrants on homeland visits but educated Yankees still enchanted by the dueling scars of Heidelberg, the porcelains of Dresden, and every token of German romanticism from *The Sorrows of Young Werther* to the turrets of Neuschwanstein. What better way to entice these venturesome spirits than by uniting the crisp simplicities of their colonial past with the casual decadence of late Art Nouveau?

　　American disciples of the new movement had already brought its linear attenuations and random iridescence to bear on illustration and advertising; and striking instances of its more practical applications were available to anyone who cared to look. In New York, perhaps the most famous example was Louis Comfort Tiffany's altar for the crypt of the Cathedral of St. John the Divine. Chicago also had its own Art Nouveau landmark in the chapel-like ice cream parlor Tiffany had designed and executed for, of all places, Kranz's Candy Store on State Street. Fully aware of what they had to sell in the way of avant-garde novelty, the directors of Norddeutscher Lloyd promised travelers of sophisticated taste suites walled with "pale stripes of gold-tinted blue—the combination borrowed from peacock feathers" and bedrooms "decorated all in white, whilst the walls and furniture of the adjoining parlor are covered with silvery leather."

　　Among these company directors was Dr. Heinrich Wiegand, whose interest in giving Jugendstil a wider influence in marine decor had come to the point that for once, if not finally, he could exclude Johannes Poppe from the picture and place all of the decoration of a new ship in the hands of already eminent young designers. Wiegand's particular choices were Bruno Paul and Rudolf Alexander Schröder. Born into a generation

The New Art.
Perhaps the most delicately handsome
room ever to grace an ocean liner, Rudolf
Schröder's three-deck-high dining saloon
(left), in the Art Nouveau style, confirmed
that, beginning with the *George Washington*, more modern sensibilities were prevailing at Bremen.

In this room President Woodrow
Wilson—returning from the Peace Conference at Versailles in 1918—took his
meals. And here his official party, aware
that the United States had not one transatlantic liner to its name, could take note
of what the late enemy had wrought.
(Courtesy of Dr. Peter Hahn, Bremen)

(Above right) A cartouche of the United
States Capitol by the *Bremische* painter
Otto Bollhagen and abundant natural light
are the principal elements of Schröder's
restrained Main Lounge. *(Below)* The
staircase connecting the Lounge with the
ship's Smoking Room was Bruno Paul's
homage to Charles Rennie Mackintosh's
Glaswegian style. *(Hapag-Lloyd Archive,
Bremen)*

Emblems.
A combination of admiration and canny marketing, Norddeutscher's *George Washington* was decorated to appeal to Americans. Paneling along the First Class main staircase *(above)* features a view of Mount Vernon; *(below)* in the Main Lounge, the White House; and *(facing page)* Otto Bollhagen's Capitol from the Main Lounge. *(Hapag-Lloyd Archive, Bremen)*

infused with a spirit of innovation and a penchant for simplicity running counter to the prevalent taste for ornamental historicism, these young men would create shipboard interiors of an originality and cohesion seldom superseded.

Of the two, Paul was the more architecturally oriented and the more pragmatic—the one who was able to act upon new conceptions of uncluttered *Lebensraum* without losing sight of the limitations of compressed space and the need for spare fittings essential to an idea of the shipshape. Schröder, on the other hand, dealing airily with the stock-in-trade of Art Nouveau, "took pleasure in bright and positive colors, in daintily gathered-up curtains, in inlaid flower patterns and gilded mouldings," and made use of the graphic vocabulary of Aubrey Beardsley (whose novel, *Under the Hill*, he had rendered into German). The result was a preliminary touch of camp at a time when most German ships were models of Prussian efficiency or seaborne enclaves of burgherish propriety. Disparate as personalities, Paul and Schröder in collaboration somehow united the practical with the *raffiné* to produce a ship in which, for once, luxury was translated into that rarest of ocean liner affectations, good taste.

Catering to the American market with that part of her decorative scheme which took cues from her name, the *George Washington* was a floating exhibition of murals and cartouches prettily depicting Mount Vernon, the White House, the Capitol, and all the rest. Otherwise, she courted nothing American but customers as open to the future as they were hungry for the past. Among these were no doubt a few who might, on the *George Washington*, recognize the well-studied simplicity of her bare wooden planes, minimal fretwork, and harmoniously related spaces and sense the affinity of her designers with the emergent talent of Frank Lloyd Wright.

Nothing like the *George Washington* would ever happen again. The ultimate expression of the persistent nineteenth-century belief that art and industry could be united, she is also the last and only ship of the twentieth century conceived under an aesthetic philosophy independent of popular taste and answerable only to itself.

SAVOY HOTEL · LONDON

GRAND FOYER of RESTAURANT

ALBERT BALLIN AND HAMBURG-AMERIKA—
"PUTTIN' ON THE RITZ"

Counterparts.
Taking his cue from a newly emergent order of truly *grand* European hostelries, Albert Ballin, managing director of Hamburg-Amerika, viewed the ocean liner as a seagoing hotel of nothing less than the grandest sort. Every enticement to be found in such brilliant new commercial palaces as London's Savoy *(left)*—from majestic salons to restaurants overseen by César Ritz *(above)*—would become fixtures aboard Hapag ships. Catering to passengers who were beginning to expect at sea what they had quickly become accustomed to on land, Ballin conceived ships to exceed his clientele's most sybaritic dreams, and he lived to see the day when, fully evolved, the floating palace would, in turn, become the model for its land-locked sisters. *(Savoy Hotel from Savoy Archive, London)*

Throughout the first decade of the century, Bremen's steamship operators remained the most aesthetically advanced in the business. Meanwhile, in Hamburg, a wholly different sense of *Raumkunst an Bord* was taking shipbuilding in a direction that would lift Hanseatic liners ever higher into the realms of gilt and glory first envisioned by Johannes Poppe.

The *George Washington* and her promise of harmonious relationship between artistry and business acumen had come onto the scene as a charming interruption but in no way as a *dis*ruption. Her young designers were soon, so to speak, back on dry land. Bruno Paul was achieving a degree of renown as a designer of furniture. Rudolf Schröder was building houses, landscaping their gardens, and filling both with objects soon recognized as a permanent contribution to domestic art of the period. Other young artists and craftsmen, largely excluded from the councils of the shipping industry, proceeded on a path that would, in 1918, lead most of them to Bauhaus or its spiritual environs.

In the absence of demand for the new, tradition, reasserting itself, began to unload its heavy baggage onto the broad decks of some of the greatest liners ever conceived—each of them headed for humiliation and second careers under alien flags.

This phase of oceangoing grandeur was initiated by Albert Ballin, the young captain of industry whose goal was a fleet of liners that would give Germany absolute domination of passenger traffic on the seven seas. *"Mein Feld ist die Welt"* was the company motto under which he worked, and he meant what it said.

Domination in Ballin's mind did not, however, imply untoward conquest but, simply, unignorable demonstrations of excellence in the building of ships and—from the executive's office to the captain's bridge—superior management of them. A man of peace whose only failing was a somewhat naive devotion to imperial splendor—in its British manifestations no less than in its Teutonic—he lived to see his Hamburg-Amerika Line become the cynosure of shipping interests and then to watch it disappear in the aftermath of imperial conflict. Unable to endure personal misfortune that reflected the dissolution of the world to which he was never a stranger, he died by his own hand at the end of World War I.

The rise of Albert Ballin was based on canny foresight, an executive imagination impelled to broaden the technological and geographical boundaries of the shipping world, and an inborn sense of the appropriate that allowed him to spot it in the shape of a doorknob as quickly as in the dome of a grand saloon. The outstanding figure in his profession, he was for years as famous as J. P. Morgan and has been remembered with less awed attention and more affection. From the pantheon of pioneers who turned a bareknuckled transatlantic ferry service into an enduring romance, no one looks down more benignly, or more sadly.

27

Deutschland über Alles.
Perhaps the last liner to look like an
"ocean greyhound," the long, lean
Deutschland took the Blue Riband in 1901,
achieving her prize at a cost in fuel and
passenger discomfort the company was
soon unwilling to pay. When it became
clear that the immense quantity of coal
required to maintain her matchless transatlantic speed would never allow for profits, Albert Ballin *(above)* ordered two of
her boilers removed and had her converted
into a leisurely cruise ship. The larger
consequence of this decision was an
abrupt shift in company policy: hencefor-
ward, Hapag (Hamburg-Amerikanische
Packetfahrt Actien-Gesellschaft) ships
would remain *hors de combat* in the pursuit
of records and would stake their reputations on comfort and ever grander notions
of *Luxus*, as this wine list cover rather
pointedly suggests. *(Wine list cover from
Hapag-Lloyd Archive, Hamburg)*

When Albert Ballin put a Ritz Carlton Restaurant on his flagship *Amerika,* the innovation signaled something more than a new and elitist way to dine at sea. What it confirmed and expanded was "hotelism," the increasing tendency of ocean liners to be constructed like the great resort hostelries of Europe. Central to this innovation were multipurpose rooms defined by tall potted palms among which harpists could be observed like figures in the fantasy forests of *"Le Douanier"* Rousseau. Much on the order of atriums that would replace them in the American hotels of the later part of the century, palm courts were the structural and decorative core of ships-as-hotels. In the hands of master designer Charles Mewès, they served to open, up and out, hitherto confined areas of indoor deck space and so provide casual round-the-clock meeting places. As a feature of transatlantic ships, the Palm Court was soon followed by broad lobbies, writing and reading rooms, winter gardens, ballrooms, cocktail lounges, and other kinds of public spaces offered to sojourners in grand hotels from Pola to Gleneagles.

"Hotelism." The word would soon become a pejorative term in the minds of critics who deplored the imitativeness it suggested, and a source of dismay to travelers for whom a voyage meant seafaring, not tea-dancing. In retrospect, however, hotelism seems an inevitable and peculiarly apt response to the expectations of the time. The ocean was no longer an avenue for onetime adventurers or displaced persons, but for a socially secure stratum of well-heeled travelers who crossed with the seasons and expected no disruption of their style or scale of living, no unsettling changes in their surroundings.

Wunderkind of the industry, Albert Ballin had become the guiding genius of Hamburg-Amerika at the age of thirty-one. Once in charge, he stole a march on his company's rival, Norddeutscher Lloyd, by introducing twin screws on a series of new ships while his competitors stayed with the conventional single screw. A matter of small consequence at first, this decision was endowed with an air of prescience when widely reported troubles at sea confirmed the wisdom of it.

Not long after her maiden voyage in 1890, the *Spree*—one of Johannes Poppe's waterborne villas—was mid-ocean when the loss of her single screw rendered her helpless. Among her passengers were some who recalled a similar incident which, a few years earlier, had caused Cunard's *Etruria* to spend days wallowing in dark waters before she was ignominiously towed into Liverpool. "We were drifting out of the track of all steamers," wrote an *Etruria* passenger, "and if the least storm broke, our watertight compartments would never hold its five hundred tons of water. After forty-eight hours of this dreadful drifting, a light was sighted. This second night our good Captain had an enormous fire of pitch pine built in a tank on the prow. This fire, kept up all night, was seen twenty miles away by the captain of a little Montreal cattle steamer. He thought it was a ship on fire and came to save one or two sailors, and saved 800 souls."

Ballin's foresight resulted in an immediate increase in Hamburg-Amerika's revenues, but still not in sufficient amounts to upset the balance in Hanseatic rivalry favoring Norddeutscher Lloyd. The Bremen fleet had speed—especially as shown by its Blue Riband holder, the *Kaiser Wilhelm der Grosse*—the bonus of royal

sponsorship, and schemes of decoration accommodating both Valkyrian kitsch and the earliest shy, tulip-shaped encroachments of *fin-de-siècle* modernism.

Yet Hamburg-Amerika was never far from besting its glamorous rival's virtues. Beginning with the maiden voyage of the *Deutschland* in July 1900, the Hamburg company captured the title for swiftness and held onto the Blue Riband for six years. In the contest for imperial imprimatur, things were dramatically changed when Ballin was invited by the reigning monarch to his hunting lodge at Huberstock, where he was "privileged to spend two unforgettable days in most intimate intercourse with the Kaiser."

Informal and country-life social, this meeting nonetheless entailed crucial business conferences. To deal with Germany's vulnerability under the threat of J. P. Morgan's determination to take over every shipping company on both sides of the English Channel, Ballin was empowered to negotiate a contract whereby Hamburg-Amerika,

30

surrendering fifty-one percent of its shares to the American plutocrat, would be allowed to retain nominal autonomy.

Successful in this back-to-the-wall assignment, Ballin soon reaped his rewards: a medal signifying his induction into the Order of the Red Eagle and, at the pleasure of Morgan, an annual salary in the vicinity of one million dollars.

Yet Hamburg-Amerika, still second in the Hanseatic race, was under pressure to justify its imperial promotion. And precisely when—in all of its Jugendstil freshness and novelty—decorative art seemed to be turning exclusively toward Bremen, it was Ballin who stemmed a tide by introducing an alternative: a kind of decor that modified the *brut* heaviness of German domestic decor and placed it in settings of spaciousness without precedent. The new look of Hamburg-Amerika's ships was the work of an *Ausländer* with a belief in cohesion as the first mark of successful marine design, and an ability to make the grandest decorative gestures and the smallest ingenuities of shipboard elegance seem effortlessly all of a piece.

He was Charles Mewès, the architect from Alsace whose triumph with the Paris Ritz was still resonant and whose experience with ships was nil. Meeting by coincidence at a time when he and Ballin were both ready to consolidate positions and expand careers, they formed a partnership that would make them the preeminent personalities in the story of transatlantic travel before World War I.

The occasion was notable for its ordinariness. As Ballin was passing through London en route to Germany from Belfast—where he had checked on the progress of a new ship on the stocks of Harland & Wolff—he went to lunch at the Carlton Hotel and took a table in the Grill which, under the supervision of César Ritz, featured the *haute cuisine* of none other than Auguste Escoffier himself. Entranced in equal measure by the menu and the decor, Ballin was also impressed by something else. His dining companions were not merely solicitors and stockbrokers but titled individuals who, in some instances, had actually chosen to take luncheon with their wives and daughters: the relaxed proprieties of Edwardian London had finally brought the "quality" into public dining rooms.

Ballin was moved to make inquiries. The new furbishings of the celebrated hostelry—its Palm Court, its restaurant, and its grill—were, he was told, the inspiration and handiwork of one Charles Mewès. Seeking him out, Ballin talked business: take charge of my new liner, *Amerika*, he proposed, and provide her with a restaurant that will duplicate the style and service of the grill. One conversation led to others. By the time the talks were concluded, Mewès accepted Ballin's proposition, enlisted Ritz's support, and agreed to be responsible not only for the restaurant but for all the public rooms of the new ship as well. Mewès would be free to do as he liked with a volume of superstructure space greater than any other on the ocean.

For twelve months, the *Amerika* was the world's largest ship. But her modest place in maritime history was due not to size but to the Mewès touch in the matter of amenities that made her the most prestigious liner on the Atlantic. Besides offering the first supplementary-cost restaurant, she was also the first liner to be equipped with an elevator.

Ritz's Carlton.

Antecedent form of a pairing of names soon to be known around the world. Eventually these names would become inseparable, a happy conjunction resulting from Albert Ballin's wish to incorporate César Ritz's restaurant in London's Carlton Hotel into his liner *Amerika* of 1905. Designed by Charles Mewès, the comparatively modest setting for à la carte dining *(above)* gives little indication of the grandly scaled but equally tasteful restaurants he would later design for Hapag's *Imperator* class of ships and, with his partner Arthur Davis, for Cunard's *Aquitania. (Below)* The *Amerika*'s Palm Court.

Master of the Grand Saloon.
Alsatian by birth, French by the exigencies of political instability, Charles Mewès
was architect and designer for the Ritz in
Paris and London, then worked hand in
glove with Albert Ballin to produce, in
less than a decade, half of the great liners
that gave "the steamship era" its image
and its meaning.

The history of design afloat is punctuated by sober moments of reflection in which marine architects and
decorators are concerned to honor the origins of their calling and, inside and out, to make ships look like ships.
The year 1905 was not one of them. As far as Charles Mewès was concerned, the problem he and his first
partner, Alphonse Bischoff, were expected to solve had nothing to do with seafaring, "shippiness," or any other
reminder of life on the bounding main. Their task was to fit a grand hotel into a container enclosing but one-fifth
of grand hotel space. Fortunately, their basic notion of luxury was space for its own sake and not, as in the view
of Johannes Poppe, something to be at all costs filled with the doodaddery of Tuscan villas, royal apartments, or
rooms of state. Their success in relating the grand scale of their preliminary sketches to human-scale practicality
was a guarantee that the first full-sized Atlantic liners would bear the Mewès stamp and keep it there for more
than twenty years.

In his plans for the *Amerika*, Mewès included what would become the "inevitable" winter garden of a type
that would hold sway until the introduction of air-conditioning, still thirty years in the future. A penchant for the
period of Louis Seize prompted him to combine roseate upholsteries with treillage, rattan with floral carpeting
and fluted tubs of shiny flora, to give the *Amerika* the airiest and most inviting public room *an Bord* anywhere. In
his comparatively pedestrian dining room, however, long tables with swivel chairs extended a moribund
convention; and its institutional atmosphere was not much softened by the minor ornamentation of candelabra,
sconces affixed to bare pillars, and portholes fussily draped by what looked like miniskirts of sateen.

His Ritz Carlton Restaurant was something else. A bright, glass-ceilinged room, it had windows on three
sides and was paneled in woodwork outlined in gold. Its chairs were generously upholstered and its tables,
seating as few as four diners, were set with crystal, weighty silver, embroidered napery, and crested china.
Overall, its message quietly informed the First Class passenger (one of some three hundred souls on a ship
carrying more than twenty-five hundred) that First was not really good enough. This open invitation to the
exclusiveness that money could buy (surcharges in the Ritz Carlton, even for one meal, often amounted to what
an emigrant might pay for the whole crossing) advanced conspicuous consumption and gave snobbishness
opportunities that would eventually turn the grill rooms of liners into elitist enclaves. Situated far aft of lounges
and writing rooms, and far above inducements to evening entertainments calling for mass participation, these
dining rooms soon took on the character of private clubs with a limited membership booked months before
sailing day.

By no means indentured to Ballin, Mewès was faithful to him and party to ambitions which had led them
both from strength to strength. With the *Amerika* happily launched, he turned his attention to a project that—
however laughable and *de trop* to later generations—would become a London landmark, the Royal Automobile
Club in Pall Mall. Then he was ready to take charge of the three great German ships of the early century.
"*Imperator* class" would be the term to designate them, simply because the *Imperator* was the first of a trio
remarkably similar, each launched within the twenty-five months preceding World War I. The others were the
Vaterland and the *Bismarck*.

33

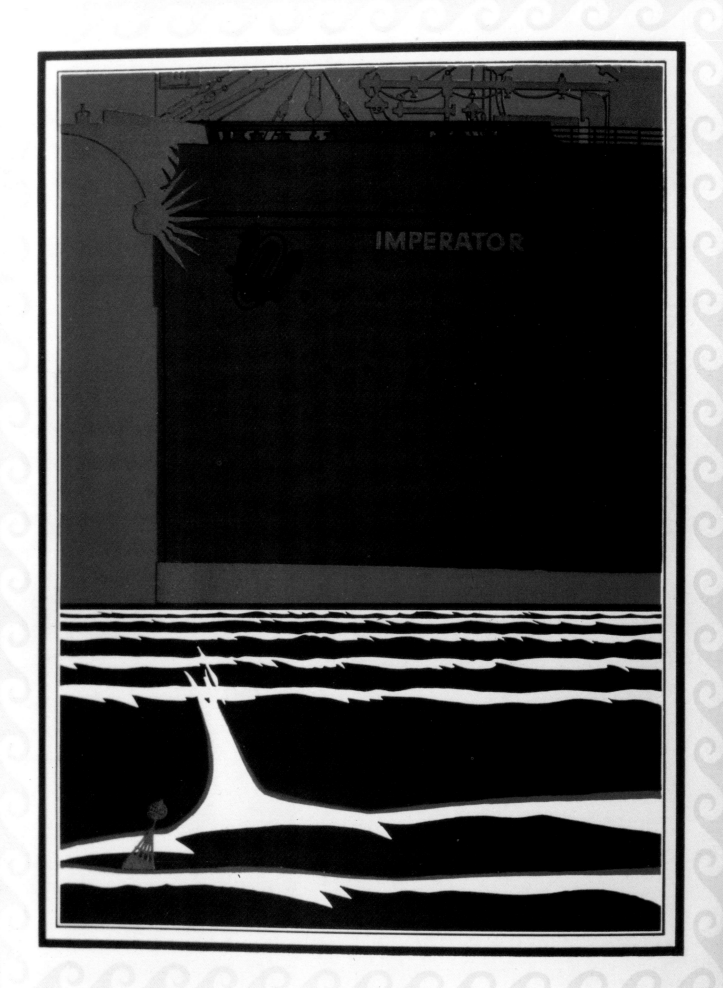

"MEIN FELD IST DIE WELT" —
THE *IMPERATOR* CLASS

Misbegotten Bird.
In an effort to make *Imperator* more impressive than she already was and, incidentally, to enhance her length in the record books, a forward-thrusting, two-ton bronze eagle, with imperial coronet, was set up on her prow. Stylish in the Prussian taste but hardly appropriate to a great liner whose mission was to join hands across the sea, this unassignably angry figurehead emanated menace wherever its beak was pointed until, shortly into her second season, at the height of a spring gale, the big bird was shorn of both wings and later removed entirely. The darkly handsome rendering of *Imperator*, commissioned by Hamburg-Amerika at the time of the ship's fitting-out, incorporates her short-lived mascot in all of its jingoistic impudence.

(Above) The outsized propulsion and steering apparatus of the 52,000-ton "monster" liner. *(Both from the Hapag-Lloyd Archive, Hamburg)*

The all but inexplicable breakthrough in the quality of ship interiors represented by the *George Washington* and, to a lesser extent, the *Kronprinzessin Cecilie* was short-lived and without sequel. Popular taste favored echoes of old grandeur and not the amorphous configurations, exotic hues, and unidentifiable flora issuing from the workshops of Jugendstil. The intrusion of the modern—reflected in wall coverings, furniture, carpetings, fabrics, and even tableware—was brief and abortive.

In his role as designer, Charles Mewès had given the *Amerika* a unifying scheme of appointments. From an architectural point of view, his hope was to change the deck plan of the *Amerika* by having funnel uptakes, conventionally placed in the middle of superstructures, removed to the sides. This would give the ship a clean sweep of interconnecting public rooms unimpeded by uptakes heavily encased and disguised by Grecian columns or Roman pilasters. But resistance—from both the executives of Hamburg-Amerika and their Belfast shipbuilders—forced him to turn to ways of making obstructive funnel uptakes seem like decorative advantages. Biding his time, he waited for another chance.

This came within a few years, but too late to alter plans for the *Imperator*. In the case of the *Vaterland*, however, he was able, with Albert Ballin's support, to overrule objections and start from scratch.

Mewès's victory was more than a personal satisfaction. Establishing his authority, he had made absolute what had long been but a perception uneasily countenanced by the industry: the supremacy of the designer over shipwright and engineer in the quest for profit. When the *Vaterland* was "opened up," so were vistas of shipboard space that designers had only dreamed of. The new ship became the benchmark for all but one or two of the superliners of later transatlantic history.

Given carte blanche and elbow room, Mewès produced grand saloons of a dignity far outweighing their pretensions and of a gravity recalling a time when the functional and efficient had not yet replaced the well-crafted and sumptuous. Today, perhaps the closest representations of his sense of *ampleur* and old order are the dining rooms of midtown Manhattan men's clubs, along with such reverently maintained throwbacks as the Plaza Hotel's Oak Room and Palm Court.

The Ritz Carlton Restaurant aboard the *Imperator*, and the Palm Court through which it was approached, were the ultimate realization of what Mewès was up to when he made his first modest imprint on the *Amerika*. As splendid as any combination of rooms in Hamburg's Atlantic-Kempinski Hotel or London's Savoy, these enclaves of international high society were not without their critics. Among these were ship lovers to whom hotelism was anathema and its ostentations a source of moral judgment which, after the *Titanic* disaster, was time and again

Swan Song.

Charles Mewès's Ritz Carlton restaurant aboard the *Vaterland* was approached by a few marble steps curving gracefully up from his spacious Palm Court. (Staircases allowing for conspicuous *descentes* were still in the future.) With this room, the master of monumentality had made his final statement. His death in 1915 hastened the end of a time when the grandeur of shipboard decoration took its inspiration from land-based models—not infrequently, Mewès's own.

With the *Vaterland*, Ballin's notion of an à la carte restaurant at sea attained its most opulent expression, if not its final form. This was no mere grill room—as the menu *(above)* for May 27, 1914, confirms—but a grand scale dining salon to which entrée was obtained at a stiff extra cost and by reservations sometimes made months in advance. *(All three pictures from Hapag-Lloyd Archive, Hamburg)*

Masterpiece Preserved.
Along with the German liners he made fabulous, every last trace of the handiwork of Charles Mewès has disappeared from the ocean. But—at lunch today or dinner tomorrow—his dining room for the London Ritz still testifies to a concept of splendor-cum-intimacy that has survived plainer taste and the threat of obsolescence for the greater part of a century. *(Cunard Line, New York)*

Schwimbad.
A kind of insouciant and slightly grizzled masculinity characterizes drawings and photographs of "cooling rooms" in the first Turkish baths at sea and this one *(above)*, with a relaxed client of the ship's spa apparently enjoying the dubious benefits of electrical therapy, is no exception. *(Hapag-Lloyd Archive, Hamburg)*

Pompeii was the inspiration for the *Bismarck's Schwimbad (right)*, with its tints of ocher and pink-orange, its fluted columns supporting symmetrical mezzanines railed in Roman bronze. If the glow of a skylight deep in the bowels of the ship was provided by the new science of electricity, no one expected natural light or could imagine that the swimming pool might be placed elsewhere—and certainly not on an open deck. *(Edward Kamuda,* Titanic *Historical Society)*

recalled as prophecy. Given the high visibility of Mewès's involvement with privilege and its prerogatives, criticism from class-conscious journalists whose stock-in-trade was ridicule was not unforeseen. Yet in the absence of any other theory of ship decoration, it is difficult to imagine what else might have so readily served plutocratic demands and bourgeois aspirations.

One of Mewès's most notable and widely pictured contributions to the Ballin trio was a "swimming bath" of resounding breadth and height, installed in the *Imperator* and never to be superseded in classical magnificence. Its prototype was the one designed for the Royal Automobile Club when "motoring" was still a diversion as rarefied as, later in the century, "coaching" would become. In its seagoing version, the pool featured not only a vast slosh of salt water to do laps in, but an adjacent retiring room in which the hydromineral facilities of the famous spa at Contrexéville were duplicated.

Pools in ships would eventually become smaller, without ornamentation and warmly lighted. But in 1913, Mewès's *Schwimbad* anticipated the marvelously fake historicism—Egyptian, Oriental, or Greek—associated

Quick Change.

Imperator, discovered almost at once to be egregiously top-heavy, with a tendency to "hang on the roll" much to the discomfort and terror of passengers and crew alike, was relieved of a portion of her heavy period furniture in favor of some lighter weight, if rather more commonplace, wicker. Then, in a more drastic effort to lower the ship's unacceptably high center of gravity, tons of cement ballast were poured into her double bottom. This further assault on *Imperator*'s dignity was, of course, not visible to her passengers, though it was soon apparent that something had been done to curb the ship's unruly behavior.

Not exempted from the weight reduction program was the Kaiser's Suite—a grand, six-room apartment with its own servants' hall located just behind the bridge on *Imperator*'s C-Deck. Stripped of its handsome, if chilly, verdigris marble wallcovering, the sunny verandah shown here nevertheless retained its serene, quasi *al fresco* ambience and a privileged view of the sea through large, tempered plate-glass windows. *(Hapag-Lloyd Archive, Hamburg)*

Passengers who could afford to travel *en famille* in suites like these needed never subject themselves to the hazards of social intercourse with persons of unregistered ancestry, lesser fortune, or paltry credentials. This advantage was spelled out by Emily Post:

"It may be pretty accurately said that the faster and bigger the ship, the less likely one is to speak to strangers, and yet—as always—circumstances alter cases. Because the Worldlys, the Oldnames, the Eminents—never 'pick up' acquaintances on shipboard, it does not follow that no fashionable and well-born people ever drift into acquaintanceship on European-American steamers of to-day, but they are at least not apt to do so. Many in fact take the ocean-crossing as a rest cure and stay in their cabins the whole voyage. The Worldlys always have their meals served in their own 'drawing-rooms' and have their deck chairs placed so that no one is very near them, and keep to themselves except when they have invited friends of their own to play bridge or take dinner or lunch with them."

with the movie palaces of the twenties. On the *Imperator*, the scheme was Pompeiian—as if to exploit popular fascination with new diggings which, unearthing the wonders of a buried city, had already led to a best-selling novel and the vaudeville entertainments it inspired.

The great trio of Hamburg-Amerika liners survived the war and carried the magnificence achieved by Mewès and Ballin into an era ambivalent as to how to receive it. For their new owners, the question was whether to consign handcrafted panels and dadoes to antiquity, or to exploit such details in the promotion of the grandest, greatest, and, above all, the newest.

Whatever, an era was over, the bold German thrust toward Atlantic dominance blunted. The *Imperator* was now Cunard's *Berengaria*; the *Vaterland* was the United States Line's *Leviathan*; the *Bismarck* White Star's *Majestic*. But neither Ballin nor Mewès would live to see the Germanic ambience of their Old World masterpieces translated into the breezy lingua franca of the glad-rag dolls of the twenties, and their sheiks of Araby.

PART TWO

British Response: Worlds of Edwardian Order

March of Progress.
Advertising the uses of Guglielmo Marconi's new invention and the up-to-dateness of both London's Savoy Hotel and Cunard's *Carmania*, an imperative message crackles from a point off the coast of Cornwall to the Strand. *(Savoy Archive, London)*

Queen Victoria would not have been amused by events ready to turn, even to spin, at the news of her passing. In the person of her son, Albert Edward, Prince of Wales for all of six years, the liberalism of which she disapproved and the libertinism she abhorred were about to replace the political conservatism and ethical rigidity forever associated with her name. Never constrained when it came to royal prerogatives in the pursuit of pleasure, Edward was now on his own, a monarch whose widely reported life and extramarital romances had already acquainted his subjects with the hedonism that ruled their ruling class and with the unapologetic shows of materialism that gave a new dimension to respectability and so produced the phenomenon soon to be termed Edwardianism.

By a fluke of history, the age of Edward, simply on its own momentum, would last four years longer at sea than it did on land—years during which its premises would be sorely shaken by the loss of the *Titanic,* then reaffirmed in spades by the arrival of the *Aquitania.*

Two of the great ships of the early century—the *Lusitania* and *Mauretania*—would be chronologically identified with the reign of Edward VII. But the full expression of Edwardianism at sea would come only after the death of the sovereign himself. The *Olympic* would not sail until, in 1911, ladies of quality in the Royal Enclosure had occasion to mourn his demise in the elaborate bombazines, widow's weeds, and funereal feathers of "Black Ascot." Meanwhile, the *Titanic* and *Aquitania* were being readied to give the age of Edward its most enduring maritime analogy—in terms of high society, high style, and in the expansion of seagoing power made possible by the slave labor of stokers, oilers, trimmers, and other faceless members of "the black gang."

By the king's mildly notorious example, if not under his auspices, the collective private life of royalty and nobility had by now opened itself to public scrutiny. Titled persons no longer sniffily refrained from dining in the restaurants or waltzing in the ballrooms of great new hotels or, on the Atlantic, sought the total privacy that might insulate them from even the company of distinguished shipmates. The picture-hat panache and picture "opportunities" that now gave racing days and presentations at court their fashion-magazine glamour were less apt to be disdained than pursued. Society at its most conspicuous was beginning to enjoy attentions previously deplored and to regard public visibility, lately considered "common," as one of the acceptable rewards of status. *Celebrity,* a word once synonymous with *disrepute,* was no longer a condition but a denomination—a noun too new to be wholly removed from the vocabulary of opprobrium, but on its way.

Ken Marschall

CUNARD'S ATLANTIC CLASSICS—
LUSITANIA AND *MAURETANIA*

Noble Romans.
Lusitania and *Mauretania* arrived on a fiercely competitive North Atlantic scene as natural aristocrats. From straight cut-water to molded counterstern, their hulls were graceful and their four towering (and functional) stacks made them paradigms of the luxury liner.

Over 31,000 tons each and both capable of 24 knots, they were the biggest and fastest liners built up to that time. *Lusitania* came first and at once took the Blue Riband. *Mauretania*, in her debut performance, wrested the coveted prize from her twin. Over the next few years, they handed it back and forth until, in 1909, *Mauretania* took it decisively and held onto it for an astonishing twenty years. *(Courtesy of Ken Marschall)*

(Above) The cover of a Cunard Line passenger list from 1914.

For seventy illustrious years, the British had proved they could build ships mechanically without peer and run them on a level of seamanship equally unmatched. Yet, following the austere example set by Sir Samuel Cunard, the random jobbers and home-office advisors who produced the interiors of Cunarders had still to provide much more than clean cabins, dispiritingly bare public rooms, and somewhat haughty assurance that Cunard was in the business of transportation, not entertainment. But the days of Cunardian conservatism disguised as caution were about to come to an end. Sir Samuel's company heirs were ready to expand a sterling reputation for dependability to include on a grand scale the loot of history essential to contemporary notions of high style. The result was a series of ships establishing for all time the classic four-stacker image of the ocean liner and the Babylonian legends of cities afloat that that image engendered.

In 1907, when German ideas of *Luxus* were most swiftly in ascendance, the British reclaimed sovereignty on the Atlantic with an uncharacteristic display of opulence which nevertheless fell far short of that taken for granted on German ships for decades. Their strength lay elsewhere—in the size, speed, and peerless technology whose superiority still brought the maritime entrepreneurs of Europe, including Albert Ballin, hat in hand, to long-established shipyards. Their new native masterpieces were the *Lusitania* and *Mauretania*, simultaneously constructed on the stocks of separate builders—the first at John Brown, Ltd., in Glasgow's Clydebank, the second at Swan, Hunter & Wigham on England's river Tyne. Rival running mates for a time, the two ships passed the Blue Riband back and forth between them until, flat-out and sure of herself, the *Mauretania* impolitely snatched it and, for an astonishing twenty years, flew it or furled it at will.

The *Lusitania* was completed first; and no other tribute to her, or other expression of wonder the great ships of the era evoked, has ever surpassed the recollection of Glaswegian schoolboy George Blake as, interrupting his piano lesson, he went to the window to watch her first passage down the Clyde. "She came . . . looming gigantic as she stood out in the ship-channel opposite the Custom-house Quay," he wrote, "and with her there came . . . exaltation and glory.

"Was it the size of her, that great cliff of upper-works bearing down upon him? Was it her majesty, the manifest fitness of her to rule the waves? . . . This was a vessel at once large and gracious, elegant and manifestly efficient. Ships he had seen by the hundred thousand, but this was a ship in a million; and there came to him then as he saw her, glorious in the evening sunlight, the joy of the knowledge that this was what his own kindred could do, this was what the men of his own race, laboring on the banks of his own familiar River,

The Adelphi Hotel.
Built mainly for the convenience of transatlantic travelers when Liverpool was England's main port for departures and
arrivals, this still extant social hall recalls
the few years when the design and decor of
public rooms on liners were interchange-
able with those in passenger-oriented
hotels. *(Savoy Archive, London)*

were granted by Providence the privilege to create. In that moment he knew that he had witnessed a triumph of achievement such as no God of battles or panoplied monarch had ever brought about."

That "triumph of achievement"—equally applicable to the *Mauretania*—belonged firmly to the shipwrights and marine engineers of Scotland and England, and reminded the world that the collective genius of Robert Napier, Isambard Kingdom Brunel, and Sir Charles Algernon Parsons still hovered over the drawing boards on which the new ships were conceived.

But somehow the almost sacerdotally somber interiors of these historic liners were hardly noticed in a period when British taste, pleased with its own fumed-oak sideboards and brass fenders, proudly embraced domestic lack of show as another element of national character. As grandly stodgy as the *Lusitania* and *Mauretania* were, their well-crafted eclecticism was but prelude to the unfocused search for a style that would turn succeeding British liners into museums of historic clichés.

The largely anonymous designers of the new Cunarders, much to their credit, were the first to open windows. With half again as much space and natural light to work with as had ever before been available, they changed for good the expectation that an ocean crossing would consist of long days of enclosure, stupefying hours in rolling saloons, or at best, card-table camaraderie in dim chambers. But innovation stopped there. Otherwise, they raided the past and saw to it that the objects they chose were reproduced with as much care as had gone into their originals. In the long view, the distinction of the *Lusitania* and *Mauretania* lies not in what they advanced but in what, technologically speaking, they consolidated and in what, in decorative terms, they preserved.

The first of their kind entitled to the name of superliner, the two ships shared schemes of interior design so much alike that comparisons are apt to become entangled in trivial points of distinction. Allowing the *Mauretania* to represent both, an account of her public rooms might begin with a bow to the embarkment hall that provided entry not only to the purlieus of First Class but to the *palazzi* of Florence. Upholstered *sedie* set into little grottoes, defined by ornamented pilasters and flanked by mirrors, offered resting places for newly boarded passengers and acquainted them in advance with the more spacious play of Medicean bravura to be found in the Smoking Room. There, the Italian Renaissance came into full flower under a broad wagon-headed ceiling the color of vellum. Della Robbia's carved hood in the South Kensington Museum was the model for the room's elaborate fireplace and its focus of visual interest. Massive slabs of verd antique lined its sides; and its delicate basket grate and pagoda-shaped firedogs reproduced originals found in the Palazzo Varesi.

The beguiled passenger would perhaps by then be prepared for the change of surroundings, Italianate to Gallic, greeting him in the dining room. Carried out in straw-colored oak à la Francis I, it offered a groined dome reminiscent of a similar room in the Château de Blois and deep pink upholsteries that brought a touch of boudoir baroque to the otherwise cathedral-like solemnity of the vast two-level space.

Acajou moucheté described the mahogany in the panelings and columns of the Lounge and Music Room

St. James's Afloat.

Sedate and club-like, the interiors of the *Mauretania* emulated the decorative conservatism of the British establishment—its taste for well-crafted woodwork and patterned upholstery, its abhorrence of anything overdone or remotely imaginative. *Mauretania's* First Class Lounge and Music Room is depicted here with exacting fidelity to architectural detail but considerable license in rendering the decorator's rather conservative color scheme. The newspaper being read by a lady passenger suggests the beginning of a voyage and an uneasy hold on privacy. But in the enforced intimacy of the next six days, one way or the other, the grand piano can surely be counted on to break the ice. *(Mark D. Warren Collection)*

reminiscent of its counterpart in the Petit Trianon. This indication of French influence was furthered by hangings of Louis XVI tapestries between no less than sixteen pilasters of *fleur-de-pêche* marble with capitals and bases of ormolu.

What all this alien antiquarianism had to do with an exemplary product of English marine technology remained unquestioned. But in the private suites of the *Mauretania*, at least, native tradition asserted itself in authentic echoes of Sheraton, Chippendale, Adam; and in the Veranda Café, where topiary art in wooden tubs suggested illustrations from *Alice in Wonderland* or the outer edges of the maze at Hampton Court.

Progenitors, the *Lusitania* and *Mauretania* would come to be regarded as unignorable yet unspectacular representatives of the class of supership they introduced. Time has dimmed their memory, and contemporary perspective, narrowed by distance, has reduced them to names which, like the names of kings, do little more than fill out a historical sequence. What is lost is the wonder, even the unspecified terror, these fabulous marine artifacts brought to an age when half the traffic in the streets was made up of horse-drawn conveyances, when

Cunard Redivivus.
Mauretania's Regal Suite—bed/sitting
room *(left)*, parlor and dining room *(right)*.

Sister ships, the *Lusitania* and
Mauretania came onto the Atlantic scene
as new entrants in an expanding industry
in which every minute innovation was
trumpeted as a vast competitive advantage.
Big, beautiful, engineered more exquisitely than anything else on the hori-
zon, these new ships delivered a one-two
punch that put German rivals on the ropes
and reclaimed for Cunard its old but lately
challenged sovereignty of the seas. This
was not accomplished by turning ships into
museums or palaces, but largely by a
reassertion of the almost forgotten genius
of Scottish engineering and British seamanship that made the *Mauretania*, in
particular, the avatar and model of ocean
carriers for nearly three decades.

The cheese-paring hand of Samuel
Cunard was no longer evident in the
appointments of either of these new ships,
yet their interiors continued to show a
conservatism much at odds with Edwardian flamboyance. This appealed to a
stratum of Anglo-American society that
was uneasy about frippery, especially when
it came from the Continent, and that still
lived by codes of dress and decorum
maintained throughout the age of Victoria.
For British travelers, the jumble of decorative styles and period piece reproductions aboard the *Lusitania* and *Mauretania*
was a comforting extension of home. For
Anglophile Americans, to cross the gangplank into rectory parlor gentility and
clubroom silence was to be assured that all
was well with that erudite little world that
reached from the Bulfinch crescents of
Boston to those of London's John Nash.
*(Both illustrations from the Mark D. War-
ren Collection)*

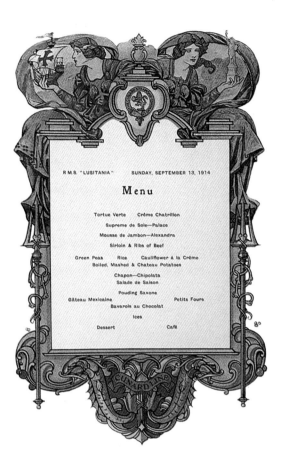

May Day.
Just after lunch on a bright spring afternoon—less than eight months after this
menu was set before passengers preparing
for disembarkation in Liverpool next
day—the *Lusitania*, struck by a single
torpedo from Unterseeboot-20, sank in
shallow water off the southeast coast of
Ireland with the loss of nearly twelve
hundred lives.

Virtually identical in their internal spatial arrangements, *Lusitania* and
Mauretania differed in "personality" only
by the influences of period decor.
Mauretania was the more sober, with a
dignified François Premier motif in her
dining saloon. Her ill-fated sister, brighter
and prettier, offered a white-frosted, double-tiered Louis Seize dining room remembered with delight in the memoirs of
nearly everyone who survived her abrupt
demise. *(Mark D. Warren Collection)*

City Lights.
A dazzling apparition, the *Mauretania*
makes a nighttime call at Cherbourg.

milk was delivered by hand, and running water was still an unexamined miracle. What laymen vaguely felt was articulated for them by Keble Chatterton, the most eminent chronicler of ocean liner progress in the early part of the century: "And so we come to these two leviathans which form, without exception, the most massive, the fastest, and the most luxurious ships that ever crossed the ocean. Caligula's galleys, which were wondrously furnished with trees, marbles and other luxuries which ought never to desecrate the sweet, dignified character of the ship, were less sea-craft than floating villas exuding decadence at every feature. There are some characteristics of the *Mauretania* and *Lusitania*, with their lifts, their marbles, curtains, ceilings, trees, and other expressions of twentieth-century luxury, which, while appreciated by the landsman and his wife, are nauseating to the man who loves the sea and its ships for their own sakes, and not for the chance of enjoying self-indulgence in some new form. But whichever way you regard them, from whatever standpoint you choose, there are no standards whatsoever by which to judge them.

"Cover them with tier upon tier of decks, scatter over them a forest of ventilators, roofs and chimneys, till they look like the tops of a small town; fill them inside with handsome furniture, line their walls with costly decorations; throw in a few electric cranes, a coal mine, seven restaurants, the population of a large-sized village and a good many other things besides; give them each a length equal to that of the Houses of Parliament, a height greater than the buildings in Northumberland Avenue, disguise them in any way you please, and for all that these are ships, which have to obey the laws of Nature, of the Great Sea, just as the first sailing ship and the first Atlantic Steamship had to show their submission. I submit that to look upon these two ships as mere speed-manufacturers engaged in the record industry, as palatial abodes, or even as dividend-earners is an insult to the brains that conceived them, to the honourable name of 'ship' which they bear."

WHITE STAR ASCENDING—
THE *OLYMPIC* CLASS

Type and Archetype.
If the steamship era has an eponymous liner, White Star's flagship of 1910 may well be the one—stokehole to verandah suite—to make irrefutable claims.

Some of Manhattan's first skyscrapers were inevitable candidates for comparisons emphasizing the dimensions of the *Olympic* class of ship. *(Above)* The Metropolitan Life Tower defers to the Woolworth Building but both are humbled by the four-stacked pride of White Star Line. *(Both, Frank Trumbour Collection)*

The *Lusitania* and *Mauretania* made the ships of Cunard once more those against which performance was measured and standards of sea-keeping maintained. But speed and size were rapidly becoming secondary to the sybaritic delights of voyages that were less like "an emphatic zero in the sum of one's better experience," in the opinion of Henry James, and more like leisurely sojourns in resort hotels. Albert Ballin had been the first to perceive a shift in public favor putting ambience ahead of expedition. Now a group of British shipping tycoons, in cahoots with an American magnifico, were about to follow suit and give the flamboyance of the age of Edward VII its full maritime expression.

One evening in 1907, a Mercedes tonneau—with a body adapted from a version of the nineteenth-century royal carriage known as *Roi de Belge*—pulled up to a London town house. In a few moments, J. Bruce Ismay, head of the White Star Line (about to set in motion events that would make him a social pariah and living ghost, i.e., his survival of the *Titanic* disaster after which public opinion, inflamed by journalists, caused him to be pilloried as the dastardly tycoon who had saved himself at the expense of the hundreds of impoverished women and children who drowned, "like rats," in the flooded dormitories of the ship he owned and so could abandon with insolent indifference), followed his wife into the automobile attended by a chauffeur liveried in green and gold, who drove them the short distance to Downshire House, Belgrave Square. This was the residence of Lord Pirrie, director of the shipbuilding firm of Harland & Wolff and host to the evening's intimate dinner party. When the meal was over, the social occasion became the business conference it was designed to be. Over Havanas and snifters of Napoleon, these ambitious leaders of the shipping world sketched and doodled plans to challenge those Albert Ballin had announced in regard to his three new superships, and to overwhelm Cunard with notions of sumptuousness beside which the vaunted speed of the *Lusitania* and *Mauretania* would be the most minor of advantages.

Working with J. Pierpont Morgan, they would build three ships, each of them half again as large as the new Cunarders. Tonnages would be fixed at 45,000 to 55,000, and the four tall funnels of each ship would repeat on a visibly gargantuan scale the powerful dignity of the *Mauretania* and *Lusitania*. They would be christened, in succession, *Olympic*, *Titanic*, *Britannic*, or—as cynical rumor would soon have it—*Olympic*, *Titanic*, *Gigantic*.

First to be launched, the *Olympic* was quick to sail into Southampton Water, there to show off the awesome dimensions and elevation of style enhancing Great Britain's efforts to anticipate the best that the behemoths of Albert Ballin's *Imperator* class might offer. Favored by order of precedence, the *Olympic* swiped most of the

"OLYMPIC"
TURKISH BATH.

Cooling Room.
The late-nineteenth-century vogue of Islamic decor, which called for a "Turkish corner" or a "Moorish den" in almost every other house of stylistic pretension in the United States and Great Britain, was still lively when, in May 1911, *Titanic* was launched with a Near Eastern retreat (identical to this one, *above right*, from the *Olympic*) for the comfort of overindulged passengers. *(Frank Trumbour Collection)*

Fascination with the "unsinkable" *Titanic* has never waned since her fateful encounter with an iceberg off Newfoundland on the night of April 14, 1912. *(Above)* One of a series of recent paintings by Italian graphic artist Flavio Costantini, in which decorative aspects of the *Titanic* are formalized without obscuring their sources in actuality. *(Courtesy of Flavio Costantini, Genoa)*

The Persistence of Wicker.
An essential element of shipboard furnishing, fanciful wickerwork, usually in settings enclosed by treillage, helped support the illusion for poor sailors that the view of the sea through elegantly arched windows showed a lily pond and not the tempestuous Atlantic. *(Frank Trumbour Collection)*

"OLYMPIC"
VERANDAH CAFÉ.

Sea-lane Club Land.

Still an exclusive masculine sanctuary at the end of Edward VII's otherwise socially emancipating reign, the Smoking Room—like this one *(above right)* on the *Olympic*—took its decorative cue from men's clubs like London's Boodle's or White's and their counterparts on New York's upper Fifth Avenue. Expansive proportions and the sobriety of dark, carefully crafted woodwork, along with a studied eclecticism in detail, reflect the formality of late Edwardian opulence. In this identical setting aboard *Titanic*, Edward Andrews, designer of all three *Olympic* class ships, was observed at about one A.M. in the morning of April 15, 1912. Sipping brandy while steadying himself against the marble mantel of the electric grate, he watched the Axminster-covered deck beneath him gradually assume a precipitate angle that would not be righted until the ship came to rest on the ocean floor. *(Courtesy of Edward Kamuda,* Titanic *Historical Society)*

(Below) Olympic*'s sunny Reading and Writing Room ran athwartships and provided a generous bowed-window alcove on the Promenade Deck, port and starboard. (Frank Trumbour Collection)*

"OLYMPIC"
READING AND WRITING ROOM.

Accommodation.

Titanic's First Class staterooms and suites were designed to avoid any intrusion of the structural or mechanical elements that make a ship a ship. Period styles, painstakingly rendered down to the carved moldings of the hardwood paneling covering the steel bulkheads, were numerous and only now and then replicated. No flourish of style or hand-turned detail of woodcraft that might meet the expectations of sophisticated passengers was omitted.

The day would come when wall-hung pallets, convertible to sofas by day, and bulkheads faced with sheets of unidentifiable material would be routinely accepted by travelers unfazed by life aboard a machine-at-sea . . . but not yet.

(Opposite page) An Empire-style suite features sleigh beds set high enough above the carpeted deck to allow for stowage of trunks "Wanted on the Voyage." *(Courtesy of Edward Kamuda*, Titanic *Historical Society)*

(Right) A confection in the Georgian taste has ocean views for those who might breakfast while ensconced in horsehair and goose down. *(Frank Trumbour Collection)*

publicity that would have otherwise been shared with her equally newsworthy sister ship. Consequently, the *Titanic* was one of the least photographed of liners, except by amateurs. Since her interiors duplicated those of the *Olympic*, accounts of the aborted career of the *Titanic* have had to depend for illustrative purposes largely upon graphic representations of the earlier ship.

In any case, both were triumphs of a rampant historicism not to be superseded in marauding exuberance until the art-laden *Aquitania* would cross the water like a wing of the British Museum somehow pulled from its mooring. The only difference was a feature attractive to the most spendthrift of passengers—a larger allotment of space on the *Titanic*'s Promenade Deck to cabins *de luxe*, including suites with access to their own private, closed-off segments of that deck.

As still another season on the Great Circle route was approaching, the London *Standard* was in a mood to handicap ocean racers as though they were entries in the Grand National. "To the battle of Transatlantic passenger service," said the *Standard*, "the *Titanic* adds a new and important factor, of value to the aristocracy and the plutocracy. . . . With the *Mauretania* and the *Lusitania* of the Cunard, the *Olympic* and *Titanic* of the White Star, the *Imperator* and *Vaterland* of the Hamburg-American in the fight . . . there will be a scent of battle all the way from New York to the shores of this country—a contest of sea giants in which the *Titanic* will doubtlessly take high honours."

THE CROSSING AS A SOCIAL EVENT— R. M. S. *TITANIC*

Light and Shadow in Southampton Water.
A newly minted "wonder of the modern world," R.M.S. *Titanic*—46,329 gross registered tons, 883 feet long, three functional stacks and one for effect—moves confidently seaward. In this evocative painting by the English watercolorist Laurence Bagley, commissioned to commemorate the seventieth anniversary of *Titanic*'s maiden voyage, we see the high profile and broad beam which distinguished the three mammoth liners of the *Olympic* class. *(Courtesy of the Darius & Nordon Art Co., Ltd., Romsey, England)*

We're Sailing Tomorrow.
An evening in the dining room of London's Savoy Hotel *(above)* provided transatlantic passengers with the most congenial of transitions between the grand hotels and spas of the Continent and the Main Deck suites of the new *Titanic*. *(Savoy Hotel Archive, London)*

The maiden voyage of the White Star liner *Titanic*, set to begin on April 10, 1912, was an event on the international social calendar nicely timed and particularly well attended. The fitness of the new ship to meet the expectations of well-traveled passengers had been established by the instant success of her running mate, the *Olympic*, and there was little doubt that she was herself being primed to assume preeminence as the Company's showpiece.

At the time, frequent and constant voyagers tended to base choice of ship on their degree of acquaintance with her captain. Consequently, news that convivial E. J. Smith would be making valedictory out-and-back crossings in command of the *Titanic* was especially persuasive to those who knew him—among them American Henry Adams, who'd booked "another extravagant apartment" for the first eastward voyage. Sorry to see the captain go, those who had sat at his table on the now out-of-commission *Majestic* and had rejoined him on the *Olympic* were looking forward to a farewell dinner arranged for the fourth night out and already oversubscribed. Word that J. Pierpont Morgan would occupy the owner's suite, and that Guglielmo Marconi, Henry Clay Frick, Alfred Gwynne Vanderbilt, and Lord Pirrie himself would be housed in similarly opulent quarters gave further assurance that the *Titanic* was on the mark. As it turned out, Morgan would decide he was more in need of "the cure" than a transitory sea-cure, and went to Aix-les-Bains. Each for reasons of his own, Frick, Vanderbilt, Marconi, and Lord Pirrie would also change their minds. But those of comparable eminence who'd booked passage would not have wavered, even had they known of these last-minute defections. The maiden voyage of the *Titanic* simply could not have been more conveniently scheduled.

Another season on the Riviera—a generation before sun-cultism would extend that social interlude into high summer—was over. London was catching its breath between the court season and a sunnier one calling for wardrobes appropriate to Ascot, Henley, Goodwood, and Cowes. Americans who'd made their annual pilgrimages to the gaming rooms of "Monte," the drawing rooms of Mayfair, and the Parisian shrines of Worth, Patou, and Cartier were on their way back.

One hundred ninety families booked First Class on the *Titanic*. With them came a retinue of twenty-three lady's maids, eight valets, a large number of governesses, and an assortment of amanuenses not all of whom could easily be classified. In the case of Benjamin Guggenheim, these included a lady companion of duties unspecified, along with a male secretary and a chauffeur.

In 1912, family income in the United States averaged, annually, less than one thousand dollars. Many of

those on the *Titanic* paid well over four times that much to occupy suites on a ship built, said an editorial, "for the financial giants of our time . . . who could lightly pay for this single voyage the year's upkeep of ten British families."

These inveterate travelers were of course acquainted with the *Olympic*, the *Mauretania*, and the *Kronprinzessin Cecilie*. They looked for nothing on the *Titanic* they hadn't seen, anticipated no service they did not take for granted. Still, some of them were beguiled to find that cabin stewards they knew from earlier White Star crossings had been assigned to them. Others took insiders' pleasure in noting that the *Titanic*'s Café Parisien, in spite of its name, had little of the panache of the *Olympic*'s Veranda and Palm Court, or that her dining room was enhanced by the soft carpeting which the linoleum-laid *Olympic*'s sorrily lacked.

But the real test of the new ship lay not in her fittings but in her social *ton*. By midnight of the first day out, when the Cherbourg contingent had been embarked and the ship's complement was minus only the few bog-trotting Irish who would cross the Third Class gangplank in Queenstown the next day, Philadelphians had assessed the range of acceptable acquaintance with as much dubiety as had New Yorkers.

Just how far, they wondered, should they be prepared to extend the pleasure of their company to the likes of Mr. Clarence Moore of Washington, D.C., identified only as a "traveling Master of Hounds" . . . to a certain Mrs. Churchill Candee who'd been to Paris to comfort a son recovering from, of all things, a "crash" in a flying machine . . . to assertively jovial Vice-Commodore Peuchen of the Royal Canadian Yacht Club—"In Toronto, isn't it?" . . . to that Mrs. Charlotte Drake M. Cardeza, out of nowhere, with her fourteen trunks and four suitcases? Wasn't she, like her suspiciously liberated name, a bit much? (Indeed she was, as the White Star Line came to recognize when her listing of losses presented the company with claims amounting to more than a quarter of a million dollars.)

(Launch admission ticket, Frank Trumbour Collection)

As for the John Jacob Astors, no one knows what they did for the next four days except to make common cause with the merrily arriviste Mrs. J. J. "Molly" Brown from Denver (who'd been to stay with them in Egypt). But aware of opportunity for social rehabilitation, the ostracized couple may well have seized it. Their marriage had been a scandal. Divorced for less than two years, Astor had up and married Madeleine Force, a teenager even younger than his own son, Vincent. Their wedding in the summertime pomp of Newport had gone well enough; but back in Manhattan after a West Indies honeymoon, Astor had found that hopes of opening his Fifth Avenue mansion under new auspices were met by the cold shoulders of a Four Hundred loyal to the memory of Caroline, his illustrious and beloved mother. Contemplating a vestibule table empty of calling cards, the Astors decided that a winter abroad might be advisable, and so had booked a December passage on the *Olympic* to France and continued on to Cairo.

There, chance may have provided an encounter with their shipmates-to-be on the *Titanic*—the Henry Sleeper Harpers, whose fortune came from the famous publishing house of Harper and Brothers. Henry, inseparable from his Pekingese, Sun Yat-sen, had chosen to make the maiden voyage with his wife and still another pet, a dragoman of striking handsomeness he had encountered in Cairo and decided to keep—with what degree of toleration on the part of Mrs. Harper remains obscure.

Egypt, Cap Martin, Baden-Baden, Menton, Nice behind them, some of the upper crust had come to the upper decks of the *Titanic* by way of Paris's Ritz or Lutetia on one of the Trains Transatlantiques running from the Gare du Nord to Cherbourg; others by way of London's Savoy, Ritz, or Carlton on the Boat Train from Waterloo to Southampton Docks. When they all converged in the social amphitheater of the greatest of ships as she headed down the English Channel, surprises in store were not so much a matter of what, but *who*.

An envious shipmate, fortunate enough to have memories, recalled sailing day. "No one consulted the Passenger List," she said. "They met on deck as one great happy family." And so they did, as Washington Augustus Roebling, the steel heir who'd completed the Brooklyn Bridge, greeted Arthur Ryerson, the steel magnate; as James Clinch Smith, of a social milieu extending from upper Fifth Avenue to the *XVI\`eme Arrondissement*, shook hands with the George Wideners; as John B. Thayer, second vice-president of the Pennsylvania Railroad, recognized Washington Dodge, the banker; as Isidor Straus, who'd made R. H. Macy and Company the most famous of department stores, joined patriarch Benjamin Guggenheim for a cigar in the Smoking Room; and as Sir Cosmo and Lady Duff Gordon, traveling as "Mr. and Mrs. Morgan," winked at the Countess of Rothes and her cousin Gladys Cherry. Whatever it was that prompted Lady Duff Gordon to assume another name, her hope of anonymity was not likely to be realized. Anyone remotely *au courant* knew that she was the couturière Lucile, with showrooms in London and New York, and the sister of Elinor Glyn, who'd written the notorious novel *Three Weeks* and was now the mistress of Lord Curzon.

Unspoken but well understood, the point of these Promenade Deck reunions was a matter of tribal circle-drawing: to establish ties that would keep those bound by them insulated from the catchall of the Passenger List

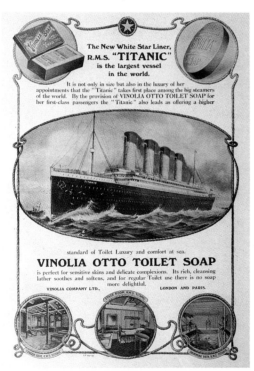

and the importunities of those who, like Emily Post's perpetually afloat "Richan Vulgar," might mistakenly regard a passage ticket as a *carte d'entrée* into social realms at sea denied to them on land. At the conclusion of the voyage, without missing a beat in the rhythm and round of established habit, these shipmates of a stripe expected to disembark into waiting landaus and saloon cars and be chauffeured to their homes, to suites at Delmonico's or the Waldorf or, as in the case of the Wideners, Thayers, and Charles Hayses, to private Pullmans ready to speed them from Grand Central northward or, via the Pennsylvania Railroad's terminus in Jersey City, toward the environs of Rittenhouse Square.

In the event, most of the women would make landfall; but not until they had endured a night in the clammy pods of lifeboats and had been hauled aboard the Cunard Samaritan ship *Carpathia*. Most of the men would not—partly because of the rule of Women and Children First, but also because of opportunities lost to those determined to stay within their own charmed circle. It took hours for the *Titanic*'s jeopardy to become impossible to ignore. When evidence was clear, by what coincidence were the first families of New York and Philadelphia to be found sticking together and waiting for Lifeboat Number 4? Did habit allow them no recourse but the security of their own crowd? In any case, they met in extremity as they had met on sailing day and so were spared having to split up and take their chances with hoi polloi from E-Deck, Omaha, or God knows where.

Lifeboat Number 4—claimed by, and so reserved for the ladies whose names were Astor, Widener, Carter, Thayer, and Ryerson—was one of the last to clear the ship. Not one of their husbands went with them. Only William Carter would survive—by a leap into another lifeboat empty and drifting away.

Who was in which lifeboat, and whether the complement of Number 4 or that of Number 1 was a bit more, or a shade less, socially illustrious was a consideration uniting the bizarre with the morbid. In its time, however, the circumstance was not without inflated significance. Tabloid attention went not to movie stars, sultans of swat, mobsters, or aviators, but to plutocrats who carried themselves like royalty and, in their dollar wisdom, assumed the prerogatives of royalty. The fortunes of men on the *Titanic*—from Astor's one hundred fifty million downward to J. Bruce Ismay's paltry forty million—were published like entitlements to an order of being as exempt from common judgment as the divine right of kings.

"In a blue suit, standing almost erect in his life belt" with more than two thousand dollars in his pocket, John Jacob Astor was still drifting in the Newfoundland current when the *Carpathia* reached New York and thirty thousand curiosity-seekers came to Pier 54 at the foot of West Fourteenth Street to watch the gangplank being lowered for a funereal procession of wealthy widows, including his own. Nineteen-year-old Madeleine Force did not disappoint them. "To the wonderment of all," said a reporter, she "walked off the *Carpathia* perfectly composed." The delicate circle of diamonds she wore around her neck was not hidden by the "enormous" sable revers of her black broadtail coat. Attended by two physicians, a trained nurse, a secretary, and her stepson, Vincent, she moved at her own pace through a phalanx of newsmen and photographers and stepped into the first of two limousines waiting to carry her and her unborn son uptown.

Not all reunions were muted by grief. Suspending for an evening their roles as "sapphic *salonnières*" in the house they shared on Washington Square, Elsie de Wolfe and Bessie Marbury were on hand to whisk the Duff Gordons to the Ritz Carlton. There, at dinner, afloat on champagne, Lady Duff Gordon recalled the sinking as she had witnessed it and somehow managed to exaggerate her personal experience of the disaster. Meaning only to entertain her friends, she spoke within earshot of a journalist on a Hearst paper who published her account the next day—with consequences that would prove devastating. A month later, called before the official British board of inquiry, Sir Cosmo and Lady Duff Gordon (the only First Class passengers to be interrogated) became pawns in a game pitting class against class, the nobility of the dead against the flaunted privilege of the living. Forced to share the opprobrium visited upon J. Bruce Ismay, Sir Cosmo soon found himself consigned to the same social oblivion in which Ismay would live out his life.

The tremor caused by the loss of the *Titanic* went around the world . . . and found local instances in the myopia essential to elitist distinctions. "Even the Social Register was shaken," said historian Walter Lord. "In those days the ship that people travelled on was an important yardstick in measuring their standing, and the Register dutifully kept track. The tragedy posed an unexpected problem. To say that listed families arrived on the *Titanic* gave them their social due, but it wasn't true. To say they arrived on the plodding *Carpathia* was true, but socially misleading. How to handle the dilemma? In the case of those lost, the Register dodged the problem—after their names it simply noted the words, 'died at sea, April 15, 1912.' In the case of the living, the Register carefully ran the phrase 'Arrived *Titan-Carpath* 18 April 1912.' "

Society would never again be accorded its exemptions, any more than technology would enjoy public confidence in its advance. "Society" would become an amalgamation of elements, none or all of which would serve to define a comprehensible condition or set a standard. The gilded age had run its course. The society it fostered would soon be reduced to the endless parody of a comic strip, *Maggie and Jiggs*, or to scandal-sheet accounts of the escapades of high-born renegades for whom silver spoons were not symbols of birthright but dining utensils.

The sinking of the *Titanic* nevertheless led directly to developments less trivial than revisions of the Social Register. In memory of her son Harry, who went down with the ship, his mother established the great Widener Library at Harvard. With money bequeathed by her father, Peggy Guggenheim began to put together the collection of twentieth-century painting and sculpture eventually opened to public viewing in Venice's Palazzo Venier dei Leoni. Vincent Astor left the fortune he came into upon his father's death to his widow, Brooke Astor, whose charities, amounting to hundreds of millions of dollars, have benefited everything from the New York Public Library to low-income housing in the very spots on which the Astor fortune was accumulated.

Less than a week after the *Titanic* had vanished, the Compagnie Générale Transatlantique's new *France* sailed out of Le Havre in *ancien-régime* splendor and set her course for New York. The *Titanic* had passed the baton to

Clear Sailing.
"The complete absence of haze produced a
phenomenon I had never seen before,"
wrote the young English scientist Lawrence Beesely. "Where the sky met the sea
the line was as clear and definite as the
edge of a knife, so that the water and the
air never merged gradually into each other
. . . but each element was so exclusively
separate that where a star came low down
in the sky near the clear-cut edge of the
waterline, it still lost none of its brilliance." (Courtesy of the Atlantic Companies, New York)

a ship much smaller and yet, deck to deck, far more magnificent than herself. That gesture, posthumous as it was, continued a *concours d'élégance* on the North Atlantic that would not end for another fifty years.

By then, crossings were social events only for those passengers who persisted in holding to shipboard protocol or those who, within the space of five days, attempted to create cliques of like-minded souls attuned to its premises. In the final years of the *Queen Elizabeth*, for instance, the Captain's Reception had become an occasion of uneasy gaiety and an index to despair. The ladies and gentlemen of the First class would, by custom, dress up for the second-night-out assembly that signified the social beginning of the voyage. When they had lifted their third curl of smoked salmon and their fourth dry martini from the salvers held out to them, Commander Geoffrey Thrippleton Marr himself would mount a dais and tap his glass. In a set speech regular voyagers were soon used to, he would congratulate them—first, for having chosen the sea over the sky; then for the charming carelessness about money that had brought them entrée into the great lounge that evening; finally, for the good taste that had led them to choose Cunard. There would always be a few people like them, he suggested, lovers of life on the ocean wave and devotees of Beluga caviar, who would resist being hurried into metal cylinders and sent soaring across the Atlantic just for the sake of "saving" a few days. At these notably unprophetic words, the company would clap hands and cheer. As "Bravo!" and "Hear! Hear!" rose among the great pillars, one could hear the echoes of gladiators in the Colosseum. *Morituri,* said the blue-haired ladies and balding gentlemen, *te salutamus.* Then, as stewards began to brush away crumbs and bring in balloons and streamers for the Get-Together Dance later on, they would all disperse. Weaving slightly under the influence of Beefeater gin, some would go down to the ice sculptures and cornucopian fruit baskets of the dining room, others up to the shaded lamps and flambéed chafing dishes of the Veranda Grill. A few years later, packed even more closely together than their forebears had been packed into steerage, most of them would cross the ocean in Boeing 747s and Concordes, and read about the events of the season at Gstaad and Hot Springs en route.

PART THREE

"A Moveable Feast": The Transatlantic Twenties

Germany: A New Start.
Norddeutscher Lloyd's 32,000-ton *Columbus* of 1923 backs out of her North River berth to muffled shouts of "Bon voyage!" and "*Auf Wiedersehn!*" Instantly successful, this modest liner, comfortable but in no way grand in the old sense, was a sign that mass marketing of the ocean had begun, and led directly to plans for the *Bremen* and *Europa*. *(Courtesy of Arnold Kludas, Deutsches Schiffahrtsmuseum, Bremerhaven)*

With the exception of liners from the neutral Netherlands, World War I effectively wiped out the industry of sea travel. When the war was over, so was the royal progress of liners catering to an elite on their top decks while reaping most of their profits from emigrants packed into the fetid dormitories of their lower decks.

To start over, shipping companies had to start anew—simply because forces beyond their control had changed the conditions under which they might operate. With the imposition in the United States, in 1914, of the income tax, and the boom of business economy in the early twenties, a conservative shipboard society of old money was invaded by free spenders of the new, toward whose good-time-Charlie expectations the steamship lines were glad to bend. The result was a democratization of once private preserves and a moratorium on rules of dress and deportment hitherto heeded more rigidly at sea than ever on land.

A second development was the passing by Congress of the Volstead Act of 1919 by which Prohibition became the law of the land and, insofar as American ships were concerned, of the sea.

Technologically, the most crucial change was the substitution of oil for coal as the essential fuel. The "black gangs" of stokers were eliminated, as were the long hours of dockside coaling when siftings of black dust seeped into upholstery, bedding, and carpetings. Uncovered deck space now became open to recreational uses previously made intolerable by showers of smut.

But the big change was the consequence of a political decision. This was the passage by Congress of the Emergency Quota Act of 1921—commonly known as the "Three Percent Act"—by which immigration was restricted to but three percent of the nationals of any foreign country, on the basis of the census of 1903. The social halls and tiered sleeping quarters of Third Class and Steerage suddenly became echo chambers.

Updated or restored and remarkably close to the paragons they once were, the ships of all nations save Germany were at the ready. But to tap a new market they had to compete—mainly for American travelers who, denied the romance of Europe for nearly a decade, were now without settled ideas about how to reclaim it.

With an abundance of empty staterooms and a vast clientele of indeterminate taste, the steamship companies needed help and sought it in the magic of the word. The result was a bastard form of promotional literature so witlessly ingenious as to rob poetry of much of its vocabulary, and to gut the novel of manners from Jane Austen to Edith Wharton. Like everything else, it seemed, high society and its class-conscious discriminations could be quite easily translated into the currency of hucksterism.

CUNARD LINER "AQUITANIA" BEFORE LAUNCH

CUNARD LINER "AQUITANIA" LEAVING WAYS—ENTERING WATER

CUNARD LINER "AQUITANIA" LEAVING WAYS—ENTERING WATER

CUNARD LINER "AQUITANIA" LEAVING WAYS—ENTERING WATER

GAINSBOROUGH, PALLADIO, AND THE BROTHERS ADAM—CUNARD'S *AQUITANIA*

In social status and richness of appointment, the *Aquitania* was the ultimate liner to take to the water before World War I. But to some maritime observers and newspaper columnists fed up with details of still another pleasure barge, the new ship seemed simply another example of what came of rummaging through the bandbox of history. Stung by adverse comment, Arthur Davis, who had been responsible for her interiors, bided his time, then told a convention of journalists what they had no way of knowing.

When first engaged to design and decorate the *Aquitania*, he said, his question to the directors of Cunard was, "Why don't you make a ship look like a ship?" The answer he got "was that the people who use these ships . . . are mostly seasick American ladies and the one thing they want to forget . . . is that they are on a ship at all. Most of them have got to travel and they object to it very much. In order to impress that point upon me, the Company sent me across the Atlantic. The first day out I enjoyed the beautiful sea, but when we got well on . . . there was one thing I craved for as never before, and that was a warm fire and a pink shade. . . . I suggest that the transatlantic liner is not merely a ship, she is a floating town with three thousand passengers of all kinds . . . and those who enjoy being there are distinctly in the minority. If we could get ships to look inside like ships, and get people to enjoy the sea, it would be a very good thing; but all we can do as things are, is to give them gigantic floating hotels."

So convinced, Davis had returned to the plunder of history begun by Johannes Poppe and continued by Charles Mewès, and, quite by himself, he concluded its term in all the lavishness he had learned to accept as Mewès's English partner. For Davis, the *Aquitania* represented a personal triumph and justification after many years in the master's shadow. For Cunard, she was a means of asserting leadership reclaimed by the speed and Britishness of the *Lusitania* and *Mauretania* and now expanded—Gainsborough Suite to Palladian Lounge—by the splendors of centuries.

Making her debut in May 1914, the *Aquitania* joined her sister ships in a long-hoped-for but never before achieved schedule by which Cunard could offer weekly service from both New York and Southampton. In operation for less than three months, she was withdrawn at the outbreak of war and sent to Liverpool for conversion into an armed merchant cruiser. When that proved to be a mistake, she was reconverted into a troopship and, after far-ranging voyages in that capacity, into a hospital ship.

The one liner destined to end the first great phase of the steamship era, the *Aquitania* sailed, after the war, into another era in which, serene and confident, she ignored developments that might well have rendered her obsolete. As class divisions on the ocean were being reshuffled, she stood fast against a cut-rate tide of

democratic *joie de vivre* and was handsomely rewarded for her intransigence by members of the old guard and some of the new. When, for instance, the young Mr. and Mrs. F. Scott Fitzgerald got their hands on a hefty sum of money from the first of Scott's novels to gain a wide audience, their thoughts turned not to one of the classless new ocean ferries, but to the best available—First Class, no less, on the *Aquitania*. "Lustily splashing their dreams in the dark pool of gratification," wrote Zelda, "their fifty thousand dollars bought a cardboard day-nurse for Bonnie, a second-hand Marmon, a Picasso etching, a white satin dress . . . a dress as green as fresh paint, two white knickerbocker suits exactly alike, a broker's suit and two first-class tickets to Europe."

The final product of a tendency toward mélange that had now become a principle, the *Aquitania* became a copywriter's dream. "You may," said one of them, "sleep in a bed depicting one ruler's fancy, breakfast under another dynasty altogether, lunch under a different flag and furniture scheme, play cards or smoke, or indulge in music under three other monarchs, have your afternoon cup of tea in a verandah which is essentially modern and cosmopolitan, and return to one of the historical periods experienced earlier in the day for your dinner in the evening at which meal, whatever may be the imperial style or degree of Colonial simplicity, you will appear in very modern evening dress."

Challenged to combine a crash course in history with enticements to travel *de luxe*, other writers assured prospective passengers that, however authentic the *Aquitania*'s period rooms might be, they would not overwhelm those who used them. The Carolean Smoking Room, for instance. Even if you were but an unlettered butter-and-egg man from deepest Wisconsin, you'd be uplifted because, in the words of a brochure, "the power of the *Aquitania*'s Smoking Room can be felt by the least erudite."

If, on the other hand, you were someone already aware of the darker turns of ecclesiastical history, you might be enthralled, since the Smoking Room "is said to recall Jesuits whispering their 'dark secret of the warming pan'—dimly heard by 'men whose ears had been torn away by the hangman's blunted shears.' " In any case, you would be constantly assured that you were at sea in a rolling "Temple of Taste in general and of Anglo-Saxon art in particular."

When the *Aquitania* was able to resume regular crossings from Southampton to New York in June 1919, her reputation, like that of many another monument to national pride, was subject to a wave of postwar cynicism. Descriptions meant to evoke awe were met with smirks. Who wanted to cross the ocean in a pastiche of the British Museum? Aware of this resistance, at least one copywriter put aside the lexicon of hyperbole and told it straight. "Architecturally," he said, "the great public rooms of the *Aquitania* can be taken as seriously as you like. In them the history of English architecture and furniture has been superbly interpreted, from the early seventeenth century of Elizabeth, as it is expressed in the grill of the restaurant, through the matured English renaissance of the smoke room, the later renaissance of the Palladian lounge, forward to the well defined classicism of the period of Robert Adam in the library. The dining room, although it is called Louis XVI, might equally well be the English equivalent, which is Adam, so perfectly is it in sympathy with the rest of the ship."

Measured Elegance.
Eclectic, yes, but *Aquitania*'s interiors
were not in a taste that wouldn't be
accepted in the most snobbish corners of
Mayfair or Embassy Row. *(Above)* Davis's
galleried grand staircase in the First Class
allowed one to retreat from the Georgian
splendor of *Aquitania*'s Palladian Lounge
on A-Deck to the relative restraint of Louis
Seize in the ship's restaurant *(right)* three
decks below.

Informative rather than adventitious, this was a rare kind of promotional language. But it would soon give over to the kind of brochure bombast that courts self-parody.

As the ultimate ocean liner to be conceived in the image of England's vaunted, and widely ridiculed, Stately Homes, the *Aquitania* repeated a kind of indiscriminate accumulation that belongs more to the assertion of privilege than to the reticence of taste. Already passé as a mode of steamship decoration everywhere but in Italy, the historical replications of the *Aquitania*—and the amassing of objects that would never find a place in any museum but one dedicated to the triumph of the ersatz—added up to a final expression of an idea embodied as a genre. Soon shipshape functionalism in the name of the modern would begin to strip liners of their domes, pillars, and the desideratum of exotic artifacts for which niches could always be found. Sadly, it would also strip them of an unpredictable seam of fantasy, and of the vague Maxfield Parrish aspirations to the beautiful that made them unique among industrial creations.

" 'Over-shippy' attitudes to interiors can be as romantically unsuitable as plaster swags and wrought-iron grilles," said British architect Hugh Casson. "The sturdy simplicity of the exposed trunking, ranked stanchions, white paint and deck line may satisfy the shore-based sophisticate, but not the passenger who has paid heavily for comfort both actual and visual, and feels entitled to a sense of luxury and occasional illusion."

"In 1914," said another maritime observer, "a serious critic would have dismissed derisively the mock interiors of the *Aquitania*. A generation later he would have found a change of attitude toward style, but little to recommend, in the design of the *Queen Mary*. Yet both these ships became in many ways the embodiment of their respective ages—an embodiment glamorized by the ephemeral nature of ships."

A dowager and the last of her kind, the *Aquitania* maintained an aristocratic presence on the sea-lanes long

Baronial Baroque.
Venetian lanterns, paintings of famous
naval engagements in opulent framings,
and acres of fine English walnut paneling
produced an undeniably successful "chem-
istry" in *Aquitania*'s spacious and popular
Smoking Room.

after bigger and more powerful ships had come and gone, long after airy suites taking their decorative schemes from Gainsborough, Raeburn, and Constable were but footnotes to lost graciousness. Then staterooms on the Atlantic would feature all the push-button convenience of an airport hotel, along with dining rooms as bare and banal as commissaries. Given the chance, who would not turn a corner and, in the warp of time, step onto the royal-blue carpeting of the *Aquitania*'s restaurant, claim a white table glinting with silver and crystal, and study a menu in its two-deck-high well of sunlight at lunchtime and its hundred circles of lamplight at dinner? Sneaking a cigarette in a passageway open to restless multitudes, what latter-day traveler would not yearn for the cattle-baron masculinity of the Smoking Room and its leathery solitude?

"Anyone who has seen the original carvings by Grinling Gibbons at Hampton Court, in Windsor Castle, or in the great ducal houses of Petworth, Chatsworth, or Badminton," said a brochure, "will realize how authentically the magnificence of the late seventeenth and early eighteenth century has been transferred to the palatial proportions of that large and lofty manor room which is the *Aquitania*'s smoke room. The full length portrait of King James II hanging over the fireplace between carved drops gives, perhaps more than anything else, its true and huge scale. It is a room which reflects the prodigious energy, the masculine and massive hand of that eminent scientist, turned architect, Sir Christopher Wren. It is hardly to be equalled in the most important city or country home in America."

The *Aquitania* may have been the ultimate compendium of period styles, but she was also a ship with a bow, a stern, and a hull housing the power plant that would propel her 46,000 tons across the North Atlantic more than six hundred times. The last four-stacker ever to be built, she would eventually sail, tall and handsome, side by side with low-funneled liners that could outrace her but never match her queenly serenity, or ruffle her dignity.

Fortune

One Dollar a Copy JULY 1931 Ten Dollars a Year

BARONETS, BROKERS, AND *BOISERIE*— AT SEA WITH LORELEI LEE

Except for the loss of Cunard's *Lusitania* (torpedoed off Ireland in 1915) and the addition of the French Line's *Paris* (launched in 1916), the great flotilla of prewar liners was intact, newly oil-fired, and ready for business—but not, in any way, business-as-usual.

Without a flow of emigrants to keep even "light" sailings profitable, the shipping companies one by one resorted to upgrading their austere and empty Third Class and Steerage space (capable, on some ships, of housing nearly three thousand souls) and giving them new designations—the most popular of which was Tourist Third Cabin. A catchall combining a sense of economy with a touch of the carefree, even a hint of privacy, the term at once appealed to hundreds of thousands of teachers, office workers, and other young professionals ready to make bookings, most of them for the first time.

In their hour of need, steamship operators had come upon an unexpected bonanza. To take full advantage of it, some went further and introduced a whole new type of ocean carrier. This was the One Class liner, a floating democracy that did away with any opportunity for one passenger to look down upon another—either socially or from the heights of a restricted deck. An American idea that found most of its support in American patronage, it threatened to revolutionize travel on the Atlantic.

"For many years," said *The New York Times*, "the ocean liner has served as an example of the working out of the caste system. Class distinctions were not more clearly drawn in Hindustan. On shipboard the lines were fixed and taut. Captain, staff and crew made up the bureaucracy, the first cabin the aristocracy, the second cabin the bourgeoisie and the steerage the proletariat. Today this venerable tradition on the high seas faces extinction.

"It has long been an axiom with steamship companies that Americans would travel first-class or not at all. But this year . . . 40,000 Americans from all grades of society booked round trips in the rejuvenated steerage. Sociologists may attribute this swift change to the growth of democratic ideals, but the real explanation seems to lie in the need of the steamship companies to make ends meet."

But if the new way to Europe was a kind of merry slumming, with jazz bands on open decks aft and bathing beauties poised above the canvas containers that served as outdoor swimming pools, what about the traveler who'd waited long years to discover the age of elegance, or to reenter it? Old-school passengers, wary of classless mateyness and come-as-you-are egalitarianism, had to be wooed all over again. In this, Cunard took the lead with *The New Art of Going Abroad*—a masterpiece of debutante prose encased in a hardback brochure thin as a first volume of lyrics and as rich in the fluidities of poesy as an afternoon with the Browning Society.

Thirty years before *Vogue*'s Diana Vreeland had brought the shadings of hair-dryer prose to a refinement indistinguishable from the parodies of S. J. Perelman, Cunard's own masters of language had found their metier:

"Turmoil . . . hubbub . . . flurry! Taxis chugging . . . Rolls Royces emitting Wall Street-y gentlemen . . . tall slim-hipped young men recently at the Racquet Club . . . hypothetical debutantes . . . and proven film stars. Orchids . . . gardenias . . . photographers . . . flash lights . . . Trunks . . . trunks . . . trunks. Packages from Dean's, from Sherry's . . . from ten thousand far-flung florists . . . Prelude to a sailing . . . overture to a week that, to the initiate, will be a largish bit of heaven . . . in a box from Cartier . . .

"For the initiate is aware that to live pleasantly it is necessary to consult one's own taste *before*, and not after, embarking on a given course, or a given steamer. . . . The initiate takes pains to choose the ship that suits him or her as carefully as a prima donna chooses a gown or an actress her background.

"Today, ocean travel has taken its proper place as a special aspect of the very special art of living pleasantly. . . . People who *know* . . . sophisticated travelers . . . are aware that the transatlantic week, from pier to pier, can be—*should* be—one of the gala weeks of life . . . one of those rare and preciously perfect intervals, snatched from the grudging gods . . . can be—and *is*—on the Cunarders. . . . You've probably noticed, in the Social Notes of the *Times* . . . or *Spur* . . . or *Town and Country* that when Mr. and Mrs. So and So, of the Ritz Tower or the Savoy Plaza, or Tuxedo, Grosse Pointe, or Burlingame, or Beacon Hill, go abroad, it's almost always on a Cunarder. . . . You may not quite have realized why. . . . It's simply because, through long years of catering to people who have always made an art of living and who are accustomed to the ultimate best, in the way of service, appointments, food . . . when it is more or less assumed that a certain Line customarily carries princes of the Royal Blood, and international bankers who deal casually in figures that to most of us remain farce or fantasy—the Line must, of course, be prepared to function according to their standards. The result is a constant . . . consistent enforcement (in the tiniest, minimum rate cabin, just as much as in the 'Prince of Wales' suite)—of the superlative as it is conceived, today . . . by the people who live superlatively."

Individuals whose parents or grandparents had stood by steerage deck-railings to watch their verminous mattresses being thrown overboard upon arrival in New York Harbor or those who had huddled in their shawls as the Statue of Liberty came into sight were now being asked to choose between damask and silk for their coverlets, between viscountesses and diplomats for their dining companions. Choice, suggested the brochure, was no mere option but an imperative (not without a touch of racist bias then still socially acceptable).

"To hear anyone say, 'We're sailing on the *Hottentot*, because the children go to camp on the tenth,' is a source of anguish to all sophisticated travelers. It's like renting just *any* house that happens to be empty—like joining *any* club because it's nearby . . . or choosing *any* hotel that has rooms that are vacant. How do you know you will like the club, the hotel, the town house . . . or the *Hottentot*? As a matter of fact, there should enter into your choice of a ship just as much consultation of your personal tastes . . . as you put into the choice of a

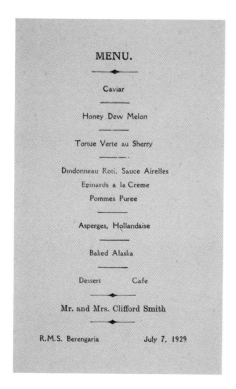

MENU.

Caviar

Honey Dew Melon

Tortue Verte au Sherry

Dindonneau Roti, Sauce Airelles
Epinards a la Creme
Pommes Puree

Asperges, Hollandaise

Baked Alaska

Dessert   Cafe

Mr. and Mrs. Clifford Smith

R.M.S. Berengaria   July 7, 1929

Home Away from Home.
Run off in the ship's print shop as a
courtesy to the Clifford Smiths for a dinner
they gave aboard *Berengaria* in 1929, the
menu *(above)* would likely be amplified by
beluga-filled swans of carved ice, tubs of
chilled Dom Perignon, and trays of ingenious hors d'oeuvres.

Classic Mewès.
Corinthian columns, generously scaled
windows draped in velvet, and the charm
of a Palm Court entrance into the *Majestic*'s
à la carte restaurant show that the master's
schemes for Hapag's original *Bismarck*
were meticulously honored long after his
death. *(Edward Kamuda, Titanic Historical Society)*

summer hotel, or a country club, or a school for your children. More: you can resign from the club and join
another or move from the hotel—but you can't jump off the *Hottentot* with your Vuitton trunks and your Hermès
bags, if you change your mind!"

The "Big Three" for Cunard in the middle and late twenties were the *Berengaria*, the *Aquitania*, and the
Mauretania: all venerable, war-scarred, famous, and weighted with three or four active or supernumerary
funnels. Without quite tipping their hands to the fact, Cunard's copywriters tended to regard the *Berengaria* as
the least favored of the three sisters they were charged to promote. In this they shared the feeling of one of that
ship's own officers, a man whose cynicism had not been qualified by his opportunities. "Everybody on the
Berengaria, even the dogs," he said, was " 'socially prominent.' . . . The *Berengaria* was principally a gleaming
and bejewelled ferry boat for the rich and titled, for the Sultan of Jahore, Lord Duveen, the Earl of Warwick and
many Cortlands, Vanderbilts and Swopes."

"The Big B" was, after all, of foreign origin, a war orphan, and could perhaps be forgiven her disposition toward notoriety, flashiness, and the kind of Dapper Dan–ism that had begun to appear in the guise of the debonair. "The Queens who cross in the *Berengaria* are the more conspicuous Queens . . . the more debonair Mayors choose her. A *Berengaria* sailing is tempestuous with the exploding of flash-lights, the pursuit of reporters. . . . Everything about the *Berengaria* is on the grand, the opulent, scale. Her passenger lists are electric with great names. Great enterprises of finance, of the world worldly, are flung back and forth across her tables. And you may find yourself the day after sailing with your deck chair next to one that rings louder around the world than any rumor of war or peace. . . . No one who is amused by encounters with celebrities should deprive himself of the chance acquaintances of the *Berengaria*."

In the case of the *Aquitania*, however, an evanescent, almost subliminal, soupçon of distinctiveness defied the rude adequacy of words. The message lay between the lines: and the burden of it seemed to be that only life as it was lived in Castle Howard or Blenheim might offer a serviceable metaphor.

"The county-family sort of atmosphere," said the flat-fee rhapsodist, "predisposes in her favor people of social consequence, people of title, people who like their transatlantic crossings to taste of that rather formal sub-division into hierarchies—social, political, hereditary—which mark their lives. . . . If a ship may be like a house, the *Aquitania* is like some Georgian house of weathered brick that looks through the mist toward the fairy tale outlines of Windsor Castle. A house quiet and beautiful with age without, and inside as modern, as perfectly appointed, as some tower that has sprung up overnight to forty stories. . . . The people who cross in her are people you might meet at an important Thursday-to-Monday, where blood and achievement both count. If you like to pack your simplest jumper suits and your heaviest boots alongside your most explicitly chic evening gowns and slippers and go down to Surrey or Berkshire or 'Bucks' to weekend in some Elizabethan house that shows how beauty may multiply by the years . . . you will like . . . the six-day crossing in the *Aquitania*, the aristocrat of the sea."

"Southampton? . . . No! The Pool in the *Berengaria*."
By the mid-twenties, the swimming pool was no longer a vaguely therapeutic kind of bath but the scene—open to both sexes—of splash-parties.

Homeric Gymnasium.
(Facing page) Uncomfortably reminiscent of a torture chamber, this physical culture facility was, according to White Star promotion, ". . . dear to the young athletes of both sexes who do not want to break the tradition of strenuous fitness during the voyage . . . that fitness which makes life good and work a pleasure."
(Edward Kamuda, Titanic *Historical Society)*

Less gaga in its appeal to Anglophile and hayseed alike, the White Star Line nevertheless had every bit as much to offer the eminent, as well as the aspiring, and could match Cunard's "Big Three" with a trio of splendid liners of much the same provenance. Its *Olympic* was only three years younger than the *Mauretania;* its *Homeric* was almost as new as the *Aquitania;* and like Cunard's *Berengaria,* White Star's *Majestic* was a prize of war retaining the spacious interior dimensions and panelings of Teutonic *Raumkunst,* now modified by a more lambent British touch—except in the instance of her swimming bath and its pre–De Mille Hollywoodolatry.

Imperially Roman, this space was allowed to keep its original character—a decision both astute and a mite regrettable. More than any other feature of the ship, the *Majestic*'s swimming bath gave rise to the epithet "White Star Roman," which was coined by one of the "bright young things" who populate the early novels of Evelyn Waugh and which, like the term "*Berengaria* baroque," provided sophisticates with a little distance between the assertions of copywriters and the claims of history. But the *Majestic*'s pool also contributed a bit of history of a social nature to its time. Whereas in prewar custom separate bathing hours for men and women were the rule, now the swimming bath became the scene of emancipated, if all but fully clothed, amusement. "The mixed bathing season opened on the *Majestic* just before the end of May," reported the company's in-house magazine, "and the ship's swimming bath was a scene of gaiety and excitement. The bathing dresses of the ladies were intricate affairs," and "in most cases a skirt came almost to the knees and then there were frills. It was a wonder that the wearers were able to keep afloat."

Meanwhile, a few decks above, Anita Loos's Lorelei Lee of *Gentlemen Prefer Blondes*—en route to Paris and its historical landmarks, the showrooms of Patou, Coty, and Cartier—was confiding her thoughts about the voyage to a diary. "Well Dorothy and I are really on the ship sailing to Europe," she wrote, "as anyone could tell by looking at the ocean. I always love the ocean. I mean I always love a ship and I really love the *Majestic* because it is just like being at the Ritz, and the steward says the ocean is not so obnoxious this month as it generally is.

"So now the steward tells me it is luncheon time, so I will go upstairs as the gentleman Dorothy met on the steps has invited us to luncheon in the Ritz, which is a special dining room on the ship where you can spend an awful lot of money because they really give away the food in the other dining room."

Lorelei's notations confirm the survival of that dining class above First Class initiated by Albert Ballin in cahoots with César Ritz nearly twenty years earlier. On the *Majestic* it was available to passengers who, believing that "this liberty is an essential part of holiday freedom," chose to take their meals in the expensive intimacy of the restaurant rather than in the dining saloon, even though the latter was "the most lofty room of its kind."

By the time the flamboyant decade had come to its depressing conclusion, "society" at sea had become of little interest to anyone but its own members; and the famous but nebulous "smart set" of the period that had supposedly absorbed society's values without being constrained by its rules was not sufficiently visible to gain the

Passing Through Customs.
Illustrator Tony Sarg captures the anti-
climactic end of a crossing when
passengers submit their baggage to inspection—for customs clearance, or
assessment of duty, or confiscation.

Disembarking in New York from the
S.S. *Arizona*, Oscar Wilde was asked by
an official if he had anything to declare.
His reply was succinct. "Nothing," he
said, "but my genius."

British Comedienne Beatrice Lillie. Lady Peel, as she was also known, contributed to the lore of transatlantica a mock torch song, "Not Wanted on the Voyage," and a famous question. As she neared the end of a voyage on the *Queen Mary*: "Captain," she asked, "when does this place get there?"

attention once directed exclusively to the Four Hundred. Instead, hand and glove with the publicity departments of steamship lines, the American and British press gave endless coverage not to persons but to personalities. These were individuals of no social standing who traveled First Class and, in their way, represented a life of glamour, scandal, and money-to-burn. Cheesecake photographs of Hollywood-bound actresses or of homegrown gold diggers whose strikes had gained national attention, along with those of dancers, divas, and conspicuous divorcées, had become obligatory features of daily papers and Sunday rotogravures. Walter Hagen driving five hundred Spaldings from the stern of the *Majestic* into the Hudson, or Tom Mix leading Tony, "the wonder horse," through the galleries of the *Aquitania:* chronicles of trivia were now given more space than the international missions of Vice-President Charles G. Dawes or, significantly, even the arrivals and departures of the Duchess of Marlborough, née Consuelo Vanderbilt.

LEVIATHAN

The American *Leviathan*.
Built for Hamburg-Amerika just before World War I as the *Vaterland*, then interned in New York and, finally, confiscated by government decree, the German ship, rechristened, became the first United States liner big, fast, and grand enough to be entered into North Atlantic competition. Refurbished in Newport News at a price greater than the cost of building her, the *Leviathan* retained the vast two- and three-deck-high public rooms of an old order and, as a "dry" ship obeying the terms of the Volstead Act, sailed under the prohibition of a newer one. *(Courtesy of Frank O. Braynard)*

(Right) Recalling the *Leviathan*'s wartime stint as a naval transport, J. C. Leyendecker, creator of the "Arrow Collar Man," produced his own version of fashion "Over There."

July 4, 1923. Casting off, her decks ashiver with the unreleased power of newly fitted turbines, the *Leviathan* backs cautiously into the Hudson River. Nuzzled by tugs portside and starboard, she sits stockstill for one decisive moment. Then, conspicuously high, wide, and handsome, she begins a downstream glide to the Battery, passes the Statue of Liberty, and continues through The Narrows to Ambrose Lightship. Dropping her pilot there, she takes the roll of the open sea and, a bone in her teeth, heads for Europe. At long last, the American merchant marine can claim a place in the annals of the great age of steamships.

Except for the *St. Louis* and *St. Paul*—two hapless and ugly little sisters of bare-boned austerity that batted around the ocean in peace and war and then, almost at the same time, slipped their hawsers and sank in their berths—American ships had been no part of transatlantica for nearly a quarter of a century.

Now, on the launching day of a new American era, a new American look on the high seas, what did it matter that the *Leviathan* was a hand-me-down, the once imperially proud *Vaterland*? The red, white, and blue of her funnels told a tale; the paint that covered the black, yellow, red, and white of the Hamburg-Amerika Line also obscured the memory of Albert Ballin, who had brought the great ship into being. What did it matter that the bill for "Americanizing" the German masterpiece had come to millions of dollars more than it had originally cost to build her? Stars and strips were flying from the taffrail of the greatest ocean liner in the world.

When America's first floating palace was ready for Americans, many of them, for the first time, were ready

Night Club.
The Club Leviathan was contemporary with a vengeance (note menu, this page): a brokerage office in the morning, it offered "talkies" in the afternoons and early evenings and a Ben Bernie orchestra at night—when it tolerated the convivial imbibing of the "medicinal" spirits which it could not, by law, dispense. But some passengers and, of course, the ships' surgeon seemed always to have an ample supply. *(Club Leviathan menu courtesy of Carl House)*

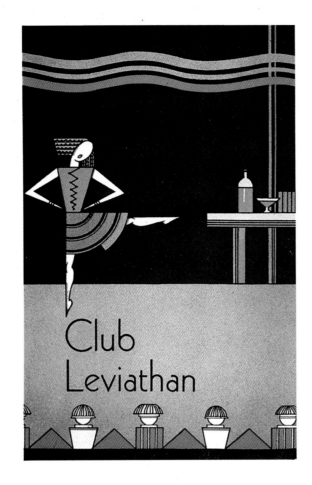

CLUB LEVIATHAN

HORS D' OEUVRES
Beluga Malossol Caviar 2.50   Crabmeat Cocktail 1.00
Terrine de Pate de Foie Gras 1.50   Canape a la Russe 1.00
Celery and Olives 75   Hors d'Oeuvre Varie 1.50
Bluepoint Oyster Cocktail 1.00   Supreme of Grapefruit 75
Sardines on Toast 75   Honeydew Melon 75

SOUPS
Green Turtle in Cup 75   Consomme Royale 40
Bisque de Homard 50   Chicken Broth in Cup 40
Cold Tomato Broth 40

FISH
Lobster Americaine 2.50   Filet of Sole, Parisienne 1.50
Brook Trout Doria 1.50   Little Neck Clams a la Casino 1.25

ENTREES
Tournedos Nicoise 2.00   Supreme of Capon, Alexandra 2.50
Escalope of Sweetbread, Montpelier 2.00
Noisette of Lamb, Primeur 1.75   Chicken a la King 2.00
Scrambled Eggs and Bacon 1.50
Ham and Eggs 1.50   Poached Eggs on Toast 1.00

GRILLADS
Lamb Chops (2) 1.50   Tenderloin Steak 2.00
Squab Chicken 1.75   Sirloin Steak 2.00
Breast of Chicken, Virginia 1.75
Lamb Kidney with Bacon 1.75   Leviathan Mixed Grill 2.00

SALADS
Lobster 1.50   Lettuce 50   Chicken 1.00   Tomato 50
Fruit 1.00   Belgian Endive 50

CLUB LEVIATHAN

LEGUMES
New Green Peas 50   Cauliflower Polonaise 50
Fresh Asparagus 1.50   New String Beans 50
American Fried 40   Baked 40   French Fried 40
Parisienne 40   Fried Potatoes 40

SANDWICHES
Club 1.50   Caviar 1.75   Egg 75   Ham 75
Steak 1.00   Cheese 50   Sardine 50   Tomato 50
Chicken 1.00   Lettuce 50

ENTREMETS
Poire Dame Blanch 1.00   Suffle Suchard 75
Crepe Windsor 1.00   Gateau a la Ritz 75
Fresh Strawberry Melba 1.25
Coupe Jaques 75   Punch Romaine 50
French Pastry 35   Petit Fours 50

ICE CREAM
Vanilla 50   Strawberry 50   Neapolitaine 50

BEVERAGES
Mocca 40   Hag 40   Tea 50
Coffee 50   Demi Tasse 35

MINERAL WATERS
Ginger Ale, C & C Dom, Canada Dry, Anheuser-Busch 60
Apollinaris 60   Perrier Water 60   Poland Water 60
Pluto Water 60   Red Raven Water 60   Vichy Water 60
Soda (Schwepes) 60   White Rock 60
Sprudel Water (Gerolstainer) 75   Cliquot Club 60
Sarsaparilla 25   Lemon Soda 25   Grape Juice 60
Ruppert's 50   Budwaiser 50   Cider, Golden Russet 60

Update.
As if to prove that America's new rhythm and image was not the sedate suavity of Vernon and Irene Castle in a ballroom but Joan Crawford doing the Charleston on the handiest tabletop, the *Leviathan*'s Palm Court *(above)* with its wicker and fronds was converted into a jazz age night spot. "Its motif," said a baffling publicity hand-out, "is founded in the art and splendor of the Egyptian pharaohs." Whatever, this "gorgeous court of moon-kissed hours"—under the supervision of the New York decorator Eugene Schöen—imposed the geometry of the modernistic phase of Art Deco upon the genteel ambience of an earlier day with a thoroughness unmatched by almost any other transformation of ship space.

for Europe. As the affluence of the twenties continued to expand, hundreds of thousands of citizens found they had more cash in hand than they knew what to do with—at least in America. Packard cabriolets, "a chicken in every pot," two-car garages, striped silk shirts and raccoon coats, "His Master's Voice" on the gramophone, and Saturday on the links were no longer viable consolations. Patriotic slogans admonished citizens to "See America First." But it was surprising how many of them wanted to see the Tower of London and the Bridge of Sighs.

In some cases this urge was prompted by a desire to broaden limited views of the world and to investigate the documentations of history. In others, it was an undefined hankering somehow to come to terms with the vague yet overwhelming culture whose emissaries—Bernhardt, Pavlova, Paderewski, Max Reinhardt, even voluble Queen Marie of Rumania—had made headlines from coast to coast. ("Any American," said one forthright brochure, "may travel in the self-same suites occupied by these great people.") In most cases, however, Americans simply looked for fun in new surroundings, opportunities to show themselves off as the big-spending compatriots of Thomas Edison, Henry Ford, and Mary Pickford; and perhaps a chance to mix with a few friendly natives. "If you talk with Europeans," advised American writer Julian Street, "it is always nice to give them fresh impressions of just what's the matter with their country and with them."

Domestication.

(Above) The homely pleasures of hearth-side were available in *Leviathan*'s best accommodations.

(Right) The lavish proportions and sculpted woodwork of Charles Mewès's Social Hall aboard the refurbished *Leviathan*. Such carved-in-place paneling would rarely be seen again on the Atlantic. Admirably descriptive, the unassuming name for this room was kept by its new American owners, perhaps because it sounded less "foreign" than "Grand Salon."

(Facing page) In service for the United States Line, the *Leviathan* became the flagship of democratic America on the high seas even while retaining three rigidly segregated classes of passenger accommodation. No matter. Ocean breezes wafting across her afterdecks are unaware of who is looking down upon, or up at, whom. *(Courtesy of Frank O. Braynard)*

Red, White and Blue.
This watercolor by French illustrator Albert Brenet, known for his dazzling paintings of French Line ships both before and after World War II, is at once dynamically fluid and precise in detail. Frank Braynard, the eminent marine historian and encyclopedic master of the career of *Leviathan*, commissioned the painting to grace the covers of his monumental six-volume history of the legendary liner. *(Courtesy of Albert Brenet and Frank O. Braynard)*

La Vie en Rose: The French Line Sets the Style

France on the North Atlantic, never a carrier of emigrants on the scale of other countries, had nevertheless offered passenger service since the days of paddle-wheelers and sails. As late as 1912, nothing suggested that she would enter the transatlantic sweepstakes with a splash that would inundate all competition for nearly thirty years.

German ships had long before achieved a degree of opulence establishing *Luxus* as a mode of sea travel. But the term itself lacked resonance, perhaps because foreigners tended to think of luxury in Germany as distributions of bulbous Biedermeier, flocked wallpaper, and fussy skirtings of *Tischtüchere. De luxe,* on the other hand—at first no more than a name for choice accommodations on French liners—became a denomination that would find its way into the lexicons of every language on earth.

Sensitively attuned to the tastes and expectations of an American clientele, the Compagnie Générale Transatlantique—or simply "Transat"—packaged French civic and domestic history with a nice mixture of Versailles and the cafés of *là vie bohème.* Yankee Francophiles were invited to view surviving grandeur and, around the corner, to experience what was left of the romantic squalor of the Rive Gauche and the neighborhood of Le Bateau Lavoir.

But just as the newly launched *France* and the still-on-the-stocks *Paris* were about to make the meaning of *de luxe* and *grand luxe* emphatically French, their careers were aborted by World War I. When, together, they arrived—the *France* intact as "The Château of the Atlantic" and the *Paris* touched here and there with stylistic anticipations of the twenties—they inaugurated a period of prosperity in which regimes both *ancien* and *nouveau* were congenially joined until, in 1927, the *Ile de France* introduced *Le style paquebot* and rendered both of them aesthetically obsolete.

S. S. *FRANCE*—
"A CHÂTEAU ON THE ATLANTIC"

Bienvenue.
Uniting functionalism with historicism, the crystalline dome of *France*'s reception rotunda *(facing page)* casts its glow on a rubber-tiled floor masquerading as marble. Modest in size, the under-24,000-ton flagship of Compagnie Général Transatlantique made full use of the French talent for making rooms of an intimate scale seem grand. *(Courtesy Ted and Joan Hindmarsh)*

Southern Exposure.
A rare sight—deck chairs in a row on a boat deck which has, in this case, been made more spacious by lifeboats swung out over the side in their davits. Even on the calmest of days, the speed of a ship like the *France* would produce its own turbulence and so inhibit conversation, frustrate page-turning, and make the balancing of tea trays with their silver, china, and pastries something of a trial. In tweeds, cloche hats, and camel's hair coats, these sun-loving passengers would most likely seek the comfort of their staterooms, or of the bar, within the hour.

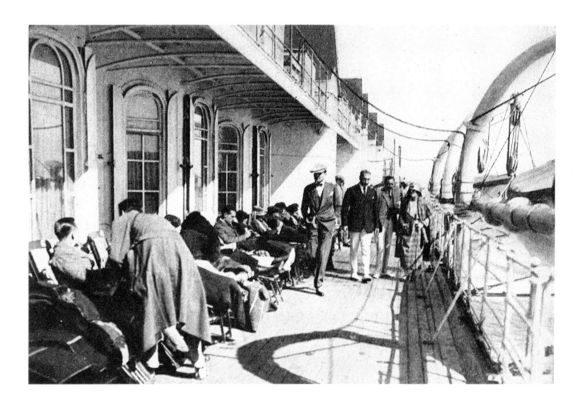

On April 13, 1912, sea-minded Frenchmen from the bays of Normandy to the seaports of Bordeaux and Marseilles celebrated the debut of the *France*, the greatest vessel ever to come from one of their own shipyards. A sober image of power, with four close-set funnels banded at the top with coal-black paint, the new liner was about to open a chapter in which, for the first time, legends of transatlantica would find their source neither in Great Britain nor in Germany. But while the *France* was steaming from St.-Nazaire around Finisterre toward her jubilant first entrance into her future home port, Le Havre, another maritime event far across the same ocean was approaching its awesome climax.

On the very next day and its "night to remember," the *Titanic* kept her appointment with a tower of ice and went into history with a seismic shudder registered in France as deeply as anywhere else. But news of the greatest of ship disasters did not impede or delay plans of the Compagnie Générale Transatlantique to put into service a prodigy meant to diminish at a stroke the claims to unparalleled luxury already made by Hamburg-Amerika, White Star, and Cunard.

Challenging the Anglo-German hegemony on its own hyperbolic terms, the *France* was more costly, more unashamedly pretentious, and, from *grande descente* to dome of webbed glass, more glowingly beautiful than anything yet launched in Belfast, Glasgow, or Hamburg. Half the size of the *Titanic* and twice as handsome, she was prepared to give the doomed White Star liner a run for her money and, in the process, to claim preeminence with a combination of French taste, *joie de vivre*, and *haute cuisine*. Ships of the French Line would soon be the invariable choice of the most worldly of travelers, and would retain their patronage for the next three decades.

The *France* was also about to make it clear that decorators in Paris were every bit as eclectic as those in London, and as devoted to castle and hunting-lodge illusion as those in Hamburg. Lavishly spendthrift, they were confident of their purchase on a native style that somehow accommodated both a heritage of regal elegance and touches of the contemporary that would soon come to be known as chic.

In contrast to White Star's adaptations of the stately home and Hamburg-Amerika's leanings toward masculine clubbiness and *Kaiserhöfliche Gemütlichkeit*, the *France* offered the irresistible romance of the château, with the golden encrustations of the age of Louis XIV as its conscious inspiration. The glitter of Versailles would serve to remind American passengers that, historically speaking, France was setting criteria of luxury across Europe as far away as St. Petersburg when the British were still trying to keep warm in hostelries with triple beds and huddling in the firelit gloom of Cromwellian inglenooks.

With the *France*, the idea of a ship as a national museum achieved its first unabashed embodiment. "Our *paquebots* are fragments of French territory which move about," said a historian. "In a confined space we produce our country: its cuisine, its cordiality without familiarity, its grace of decoration, its harmonious ensembles of color in which there is nothing too loud or shocking." This self-congratulatory encomium was not far off the mark—notwithstanding the opinion of one much-traveled Englishman who knew the limits of license when he saw them. Ships like the *France*, he said, "are beautifully decorated, and fitted with every luxury; but they do not suit British taste, inasmuch as no notice is taken of the Sabbath day. The cuisine, wines, and attendance," he conceded, "are excellent."

If there was a fairly obvious note of arrogance in the promotion of the *France* as a chip off the old block of ormolu or Pyrenean marble, the style-conscious French were entitled to it. The salons of their new flagship— Mixte, Mauresque, à Manger and de Conversations—were intransigently Gallic and just as smugly devoted to the remnants of *ancien-régime* hauteur.

The size of the *France* was less than that of her illustrious competitors for one good reason: still in progress, the man-made harbor of Le Havre could not handle anything larger. While she did not sit in the water as tall and overbearing as her rivals, in her own immodest way she packed splendor into a tonnage of 24,000, and left in her wake a renewed idea of what *la belle époque* was all about.

Crossing the gangplank of this avatar afloat, you'd find yourself in a reception hall, where, guided by page boys liveried in scarlet, brass-buttoned, and wearing pillbox hats, you would mount a staircase that duplicated in small the upsweeping entrance to the Bibliothéque Nationale and would enter the damask-and-gilt coziness of

S. S. "FRANCE"

Cⁱᵉ Gⁱᵉ TRANSATLANTIQUE

FRENCH LINE

The penultimate phase of La Belle Epoque found its proper setting at sea in the Beaux Arts splendor of the *France*'s Louis XV Salle à Manger. Beneath gilded arches, a lofty dome of painted sky, and the russet glow of a large *école de Watteau* canvas *(detail above)*, the ship's designers created what would become a salient feature of French Line ships right up to the last—a *grande descente*. This one was copied from an original by Robert de Cotte in the Hôtel du Comte de Toulouse.

The first meals on these glittering tables were served one week after the sinking of the *Titanic* and the last more than twenty years later. Then the *France*, noblest French liner of her era, had to submit to changing tastes and the appearance of transatlantic liners that her first customers would have regarded as examples of aesthetic barbarism. *(Dining room from the Frank Trumbour Collection; detail from the Mark Goldberg Collection)*

your stateroom. Dressed for dinner (informally, as first-night-out custom prescribed), you'd then descend into a dining room of Sistine dimensions and gastronomical refinement more exquisite than any other on the ocean. Later, digesting your *cerises jubilées* or some likewise flambéed concoction, and cruising the Salon Mixte for signs of life, you might decide to continue aft to the Salon Mauresque. There, stewards costumed like operetta Zouaves in fezzes and bloomers would lift long-spouted pots to serve thimblefuls of Turkish coffee in a setting so socially rarefied, according to a company brochure, that you'd be accosted neither by shipmates so gauche as to be "in need of a Baedaker" nor, to be sure, by other presumptuous persons "of doubtful antecedents." Perhaps stimulated by the sludge-thick coffee and the presence of passengers certified by the *Almanach de Gotha*, yet still out for company, you might then peek into the grand salon. There, observing the Roi Soleil himself in portraits staring out at one another across the length of the Corinthian-columned space, you might settle for an impromptu *causerie* under the light of its delicately reticulated dome. Should you still harbor an impulse toward a nightcap and a cigar, you might then settle into the Salon de Fumeur, but not for long. In this anomalous exception to boulevardier ambience on the *France*, dispiriting associations with Tyrolean beer halls would soon send you toward the more comprehensible antiquity of your Directoire stateroom. Ruffling the fringes of your fluted bed lamp, you might then say a silent goodnight to those of your shipmates still working their way through the fields of Agincourt toward the Tour Eiffel.

Durable Fad.

Filling a space beneath a staircase on the *France* was the Salon Mauresque, a cozy haven for those seeking respite from the formality of other public rooms and a place ". . . where decorations reflect the far, desert outposts of the great French Empire . . . and a silent Algerian serves his country's beverage as Americans like it best."

To all effects over by the First World War, the early century's craze for Islamic *décor* and its inlaid ivories, bulbous ottomans, and lusterless copperware was momentarily rejuvenated in 1922 by the discovery of pharaoh Tutankhamen's treasure-filled tomb. Encouraged by this development—and with little reason to reclaim the salon's out-of-the-way location for other uses—the ship's owners kept the quaint anachronism to the end of her sailing days. *(Illustration from the Frank Trumbour Collection)*

Levée.
Beginning in the Grand Salon Louis
Quatorze under the gaze of a resplendent
Sun King, the pervasive atmosphere of
exclusively French period styles aboard
the *France* was finally, perhaps, a little
suffocating. Nevertheless, single-minded
designers invested the luxurious liner with
an aesthetic coherence not widely found in
other deluxe ships of the period. *(Below)*
The simpler style of the ship's gymnasium.
(Both, Frank Trumbour Collection)

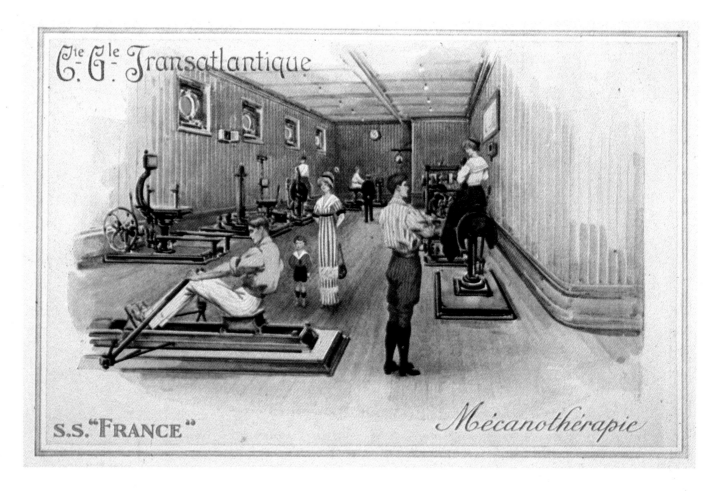

Boudoir.
When *France* was launched, her owners
were less concerned with choices of period
decor than about their historical fidelity.
As with her contemporaries, avoidance of
any intrusive "nautical" element was a
guiding principle in the design of rooms
such as this cozy *chambre* in one of
France's grand suites. *(Paul Richards
Lemma Collection)*

S. S. *PARIS* —
ART NOUVEAU TO *L'ART MODERNE*

Emblems.
Contemporary with the newly erected sky-scrapers she is passing, the French Line's lithe and handsome, 34,569-ton *Paris* of the early twenties, loaded with Americans, heads for home. *(Courtesy of Ted and Joan Hindmarsh Collection)*

À la Mode.
A magazine cover from the mid-twenties depicts the ideal abstraction to which fashionable women travelers were expected to conform: cloche-hatted, in dresses like tubes, their bearing and costume absorbed by the geometry of the setting or somehow distributed into it with the mechanical symmetry of a Léger.

All of a third larger than her predecessor and eventual running mate, the *Paris* was launched in 1916 but not put into service until 1921. Released from anchorage in Brittany's Quiberon Bay where, no more than a hull waiting for a superstructure, she had sat out the war, she became the one particular liner in which the extremes of prewar decoration were tempered by the last iridescent echoes of Art Nouveau and the first timid manifestations of Art Deco.

Destined always to be betwixt and between, the *Paris* was born in the right place at the wrong time. The largest ship ever built in France, her shape and bearing made her look even bigger than she was; and her original interiors were a dream of *belle-époque* Paris expanded to include the ingenuities of René Lalique and the touch of craftsmen who turned bare rods of iron into birds, beasts, and delicate traceries of flora.

The life of the *Paris* was dogged by events that rendered her an anomaly and, finally, by the bad luck that caused her to be set ablaze and so reduced the lovely length of her to an item of flotsam in the tides of Le Havre. Yet before she sank and became something to avoid (which the hapless *Liberté*, née *Europa*, failed to do) she made her mark as the most profitable liner on the Atlantic run and varied the history of marine decor by representing, all at once, a backward look toward Beaux Arts spaciousness, a tentative embrace of the contemporary, and a *sportif* presentiment of the *moderne*. Largely forgotten in the annals of transatlantica, the *Paris* is nonetheless the liner bridging the weighty historicism of the old and the lineations, jagged or pure, that had begun to define the new. Starting on the ocean in a hobble skirt, so to speak, she put on the beaded shifts and headbands of the early twenties and shimmied her way into the era of the *Ile de France*. She deserves to be remembered for what she was: a ship that survived extraordinary exigencies of transition with dignity and, one is tempted to think, with patience.

Her dining room was a throwback to the nineteenth-century Age of Ironwork in which anything that could be wrought, was. The result was a handsome double staircase that gave the descent of even the shyest and most anonymous passenger an air of theatricality, and an upper gallery enhancing the loftiness of a room already luminous under ceiling light transfused through scrolled glass. Her grand salon, on the other hand, was an excursion into eclecticism that would not have embarrassed the Moorish architects of the Alhambra. This room was entered by a staircase above which arches made languid semicircles nevertheless sturdy enough to support a domed ceiling as exquisitely crafted as a Fabergé egg.

Decorated in modes old and new and, finally, redecorated in *l'art moderne* as, according to a French Line

Transition.
The Beaux Arts spaciousness, Art Nouveau curves, and all-over Mauresque figuration that gave the *Paris* her original character was largely obscured when, after a fire aboard in 1929, her passenger accommodations were rebuilt. Launched in 1916, the ship was vulnerable to changing taste even as she made her first commercial voyages in 1921. Her acclaimed sister, *Ile de France*—a floating reprise of the epoch-making 1925 Exposition Internationale des Arts Décoratifs et Industriels Modernes—provided the model for the *Paris*'s renovation and an opportunity to share some of the newer ship's glamour.

Reconstruction of the Main Foyer, shown here in before *(above)* and after *(right)* views, with its elegant original *grande descente* by Richard Bouwens Van der Boijen, was typical of changes wrought throughout the ship's First Class. Indicating the advance of a style that would eventually become known as Art Deco, Bouwens's tapering standards and fluid arches were replaced by pillars and bluntly massive beams. *(Both from the Paul Richards Lemma Collection)*

Main Foyer of the Paris

Dining Salon of the Paris

Fin de Siècle.
Least altered of any public room in her
1929 refit, the *Paris*'s *belle-époque* Dining
Salon remained a double-tiered space,
majestically proportioned. Surrounded
elsewhere on board by Art Deco angularities, the room's crystal vaulting and
sinuous iron-railed staircase were vestiges
of an earlier architectural delicacy. *(Courtesy of Paul Richards Lemma Collection)*

Art Deco Deluxe.
Minor and marginal at first, Art Deco
made increasingly bold intrusions upon the
choicest suites of the *Paris*. But the French
Line's commitment to bringing the decor of
their ships into sympathy with "la che-
mise" and the "shingle bob" did not mean
abandoning the principles of *grand
confort*.

(*Above*) An A-deck deluxe accommodation employs door-height wainscoting to
broaden narrow dimensions and a hand-
loomed tapis to focus attention on a
private verandah. (*Paul Richards Lemma
Collection*)

brochure, "France decrees at the moment," the *Paris* continued to hold her own with her illustrious sister ships,
the *France* and the *Ile de France*, right up to the debut of the *Normandie*. But the effort was costly, however
nicely supported by flights of ad-agency poesy. "The new *Paris*," wrote one lyricist, "younger than ever, equipped
by her friends the French decorators with a phrase book made up of last words—with an orchestra twirling them
all into motion in the new Salon Mixte . . . this daring room takes shades of red, shuffles them with the fingers
of genius and turns out one of those disturbing, stimulating modern harmonies that make history. As the dancers
drift out across the dance floor of wine-colored glass illuminated from below . . . the walls are poems in rare
inlaid woods, the light flowing from great cabochons set in the ceiling and spraying upward from the cornice."

The *Paris* lived to see the day when—a dowager at the age of twenty—she would find herself docked at Le
Havre beside the spectacular new *Normandie*. Still game and running, she had contributed both style and
manner to the younger ship, yet could not forestall the fate that was in store for each. She would soon be but one
more name in a litany of ships (*Atlantique, Liberté, Normandie, Ile de France*) which, one way or another, fell
victim to flames and reduced the passenger fleet of the French merchant marine to smoking hulks and derelicts.

French Line

S.S. PARIS

Modern Mood.
Well in advance of the era of ricocheting laser beams and conversation-drowning amplified sound, the roseate glow of an illuminated dance floor brought a bit of electricity to nightlife in the Salon Mixte.

"THE LONGEST GANGPLANK
IN THE WORLD"

Weekly Express Service between
New York, London and Paris

French Line

Compagnie Générale Transatlantique
New York-Paris

CROSSING ON THE *ILE*

Selling the "Sizzle."
The notion that once you stepped across the gangplank onto the deck of a French liner you would suddenly be in France was at once so appealing, effective, and essentially valid that it remained a staple of French Line promotion from the mid-twenties to the end of the transatlantic era. *(Paul Richards Lemma Collection)*

(Above) Assured of a full complement of intelligentsia in Cabin Class and Third en route between Greenwich Village and the *Rive Gauche*, the French Line promoted the *Ile de France*'s First Class with images of gaiety touched with a degree of insouciance requisite to the period's notion of smartness.

Ile de France. A classic and a trend-setter from her inception, she was black-hulled, three-funneled, and as distinctive in line and cut as a Donald McKay clippership or a jacket by Coco Chanel. The first full-scale liner to be launched after World War I, she joined the *France* of 1912 and the *Paris* of 1921 on the run from Le Havre to New York and at once made her well-endowed sisters seem like revenants.

In theory and in fact, the *Ile* may well be the first of ocean liners—in a succession leading to the final *France* of 1962—to embrace the modern at the very moment when steamship history was becoming a romance of the past. In any case, she was the product of enlightened company directors and decorators dead-set against repeating even the most celebrated innovations of their predecessors and wide open to all manifestations of the present—especially as they were assembled and put on display at Paris's momentous 1925 Exposition des Arts Décoratifs et Industriels Moderne.

To the French, the *Ile* was a seaborne emissary of *les temps modernes*—in decor and in amenity as well as in the hedonistic postwar spirit which embraced *luxe, volupté*, and left the sobering profundities of *calme* to poets and the curators of *les beaux arts* and *la belle époque.* Unlike most ships competing for attention on the crowded Great Circle route, she turned out to be all that her promoters and publicists said she was—a kind of living theater in settings of Art Deco where, sleek as mannequins, men and women tapped their Melachrinos on lacquered cases from Cartier, poured martinis and Manhattans from Christofle shakers, and danced on illuminated glass flooring to the rhythms of New Orleans jazz.

Instead of appointing one designer to coordinate the decor of the *Ile de France*, her builders commissioned a team of craftsmen to work in terms of a principle born of an idea—that a ship should be in all ways a creation, in no way a reproduction. This idea came from John dal Piaz, president of the Compagnie Générale Transatlantique, and was potent enough to change the means and methods by which liners would thereafter be fitted out. No longer would ships be floating anthologies of period styles or reliquaries of national memorabilia; each in its own way would now be an original. Consequently, the *Ile de France* opened the path to a development which, at the tail end of their evolution, passenger ships were finally aesthetic objects of sufficient autonomy to allow them to give back to domestic architecture what they had taken from it: a mode and a manner, particularly that mixture of plane geometry and incidental modernism that formed the basis of *le style paquebot*.

To Americans—would-be expatriates and provincial Francophiles alike—these images of modernity were less alluring than the *Ile*'s Gallic élan combining *laisser-faire* with café sociability and a whiff of naughtiness associated with the raunchier side of French domestic life, especially that depicted on postcards never committed to the mails.

Foreign Customs.
To most Americans, for whom suppertime was anywhere between five and six-thirty, "dinner at eight" was another fancy French notion given a degree of domestic glamour by Edna Ferber's popular novel of that title and its movie adaptation.

The Transatlantic Style.
(Facing page) Approached to bring her designing talents to the restoration of Cincinnati's Netherland Plaza Hotel, Rita St. Clair made an immediate and apt connection. "When I first saw the building," she said, "it reminded me of a great ocean liner; perhaps this was how the old *Normandie* looked." From a historical point of view, she would have been closer to the mark had she noted that delicate point of contiguity where, aesthetically speaking, the *Ile de France* and the *Normandie* overlapped. Quiddities aside, she and her colleagues then went on to reproduce an Art Deco wonder that gives visibility and palpability to much of what vanished with the irreplaceable liners.

The Netherland Plaza is a reminder of the potency of *le style paquebot* as an influence of land-based architecture. In a radical reversal from the years when a Johannes Poppe or a Charles Mewès would borrow freely from town house or grand hotel to define the proper seagoing environment, architects of the new dispensation—beginning with the *Ile de France* of 1927—adopted an architectural vernacular that had evolved at sea. *(Courtesy of Norman McGrath)*

Aboard the Ile de France

The *Ile de France* was handsome without being grand, comfortable without being overstuffed, class-conscious without living by exclusions. Yet no one would ever adequately account for her matchless power to attract the talented and youthful, the stylish and the eminent; or say why it was that one ship, neither better nor bigger than a dozen others on the same Atlantic thoroughfare, would win for herself unprecedented affection and loyalty. Names that appeared again and again on her tasseled and embossed passenger lists provide an index to her appeal, and perhaps to her character: Arturo Toscanini, Maurice Chevalier, Will Rogers, Maude Adams, John D. Rockefeller, Jascha Heifetz, Bernard Baruch, Argentina, Virgil Thomson, Ivar Kreuger, Jeanette MacDonald, Tallulah Bankhead, Gloria Swanson, Barbara Hutton, Helen Morgan, Pola Negri, Feodor Chaliapin, Samuel Goldwyn.

110

Smoking Salon of Ile de France

Mixed Company.

By the time the once sacrosanct Smoking Room became the Salon de Fumeur, women had adopted tubular dresses, "boyish" bobs, and the long cigarette-holders that would soon be the one visibly distinctive appurtenance setting some of them apart from men. Instead of a clubroom retreat for gentlemen snoring over open books, the Smoking Room was now a social center as well-populated as any other on the ship.

One of *five* in the *Ile*'s First Class, this two-deck-high skylighted and clerestoried Smoking Room was connected by a staircase to the Café Terrasse, "a smarter, more amusing version of the sidewalk cafés in Paris . . ." *(Paul Richards Lemma Collection)*

Even dogs had their day on French Line ships as the above menu, "Pour votre fidèle Compagnon," makes clear. *(Courtesy of Ted and Joan Hindmarsh)*

Realized first by the French, "the steamship style" would soon be emulated in Germany, borrowed in Italy, and amplified in Great Britain. Before long, its success would start a scramble toward up-to-dateness for its own sake in which undigested notions of modernism would lead to size without grace, efficiency without charm, and a kind of aesthetic socialism which excluded the past in favor of an amorphous present. A determination to say good riddance to the decorative excesses of the early century was not enough to preclude the introduction of equally oppressive extravagances of chrome, laminated wood, and a thousand forms of plastic glossed, bent, and twisted for shipboard use. This drive to be at all costs new would not end until, each in her own way, the ne plus ultra *Normandie* and the *United States* would prove that quality was impervious to misguided notions of contemporaneity and to those misapprehensions of the modern that produce the modernistic. Meanwhile, there would be an intervening decade during which, across the shipbuilding world, Bauhaus and Loew's Paradise, Sally Rand's Century of Progress and Rockefeller's Radio City would compete like concessionaires for space and influence on the sea-lanes of the North Atlantic.

A mélange of effects on its way toward becoming a style, the decor of the *Ile de France* escaped historicism and yet in the end achieved coherence only by the same loose consensus in which a retrospective exhibition of

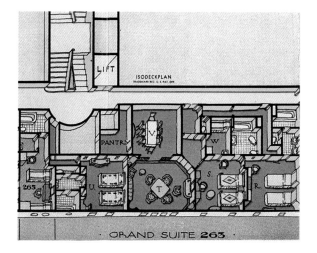

Private Lives.
"Five rooms in all—a drawing room and dining room divided by modernist iron gates, three bedrooms, sunken baths, huge trunk space, your own private steward to prepare and serve anything from a mere gesture like tea to a dinner that couldn't be surpassed in Paris, or a midnight supper that sparkles along till dawn . . ." In the stylistic purity of their contemporary setting, even the passengers seem to be products of Art Deco. *(Paul Richards Lemma Collection)*

Grande Suite of Ile de France

arts and crafts in 1925 had become the *fons et origo* of a ubiquitous international style. In some respects, Art Deco was passé before it was new. By the time it had become the scheme governing the *Ile de France*, encroachments by the angularities of *le style moderne* and intimations of what would later be classified as high tech were elsewhere widely in evidence.

Determined as they were to make their ship the epitome of the newly recognized style, the decorators of the *Ile* nevertheless had to work with architects whose tastes reflected what was left of Beaux Arts monumentalism, an influence apparent at first glance. The *brut* mausoleum modern of her grand entrance foyer with its gull-bone arches was consistent with the marmoreal solemnity of a dining room "done in three shades of grey marble from the Pyrenees." Even when lighted by its one hundred twelve fixtures of electrified Lalique, each with its own motif, this room was a vast well of space resisting the congeniality it was meant to encourage.

The *Ile*'s grand salon, by contrast, was an open invitation to roseate ease. Its forty tall columns, lacquered red and closely spaced in clusters, were proof that classic proportions need not inhibit informality; and its vast scattering of chairs upholstered in Aubusson helped to warm a space otherwise threatened by the cool glare of indirect lighting from a vaulted ceiling. But good or bad, unified and harmonious design on the *Ile*, in spite of

Le Salon Mixte.
Youth and Love by Janniot, reflected in Subes's immense octagonal mirror at the top of the Grand Staircase, is surrounded by the white ash and silvered bronze of Ruhlmann's paneling in the *Ile*'s popular daytime gathering place. Entered through urn-flanked wrought-iron gates on either side of the Grand Foyer stairwell, light and lofty, the Salon Mixte suggested the ultimate elaboration of "oceanic" Art Deco soon to come. The designation of this room was, by the late twenties, no more than a reminder of the not too distant past when ladies and gentlemen were assumed to have need of separate retreats in which to observe separate proprieties.

L'Opéra.
(Facing page) French Line advertisements featured visions of Parisian elegance and formality curiously at odds with a dominant new tendency, both aboard and abroad, toward the casual.

intentions put forth with the gravity of philosophical pronouncements, was little in evidence. Except for a working replica of a Parisian sidewalk café with awnings that brought the boulevard Montparnasse to the foot of West Fourteenth Street, the *Ile* was a rolling *marché aux puces* of statuary, bas-reliefs, paintings, ironwork, and enameled panels from the ateliers of thirty-one different craftsmen and assorted artisans. In order to "show all the richness and all the imagination of French decorative art," those in charge of the *Ile* permitted variety in the kind of excess that leads to anonymity. In this spirit, none of the *Ile*'s four hundred thirty-nine First Class cabins was a duplicate, nor were any of her ten *luxe* suites or the four apartments designated *grand luxe*.

Ultimately, the distinction of the *Ile de France* is a fact of social history or, more precisely, cultural history, in the years when Paris was the great, good place for those in search of personal liberty; the playground of madcap aristocrats from the Scottish highlands to Back Bay; the crucible of creative imagination at which it was essential for artists of every discipline and all persuasions to warm their hands. A product of the times of which she became an emblem, the *Ile de France* no doubt lacked the settled elegance of the *France* and the *Paris*. Yet she inherited all of their boulevardier panache, their available but finally impenetrable "Frenchiness," and stole many of their faithful passengers.

These were largely Americans, individuals who, never having studied with Nadia Boulanger or been invited to one of Gertrude Stein's "evenings" in the rue de Fleurus, nevertheless lived in the aftermath of great events, from the first performance of Stravinsky's *Le Sacre du Printemps* to the publication of Hemingway's *The Sun Also Rises*. These were the natives whom historians inevitably call "culture-starved." The truth is that they were more culturally aware, more intimately attuned to developments of which their own compatriots knew nothing; more advanced in knowledge, judgment, and the place of France in the world of art than most of their French contemporaries.

Whatever their hungers or aspirations, as soon as it was possible to travel overseas after World War I, a good proportion of America's intelligentsia began a love affair with the French Line. "The Longest Gangplank in the World" was the company's slogan, and its meaning was specific: to step aboard in Manhattan was to be at once translated three thousand miles to the vicinage of Le Dôme, La Coupole, and Le Jardin des Lilas. Floating academies of art and science, French Line ships became the overwhelming choice of artists, writers, composers, and other Americans informed enough to know who Toulouse-Lautrec was, what to do with *escargots*, how to get to Le Lapin Agile, and just what Sylvia Beach would charge for the blue paperbound copy of *Ulysses* they would smuggle through Customs in the false bottoms of their steamer trunks.

PART FIVE

The Italians: Grand Opera on the Sunny Southern Route

Standard-bearers.
Outwardly unremarkable at just over
18,000 tons and under 600 feet in length,
the *Conte* liners—*Rosso* and *Verde*—were
nonetheless among the first to establish a
significant Italian presence on the Mediter-
ranean-to-New York run. Designed originally for the lucrative Genoa–South
America trade, to which they reverted after
a few years, their interiors were as riotous
as their silhouettes restrained. Depicted
here in a poster commissioned for her
maiden voyage, Lloyd Sabaudo's new
flagship *Conte Rosso* makes her way to
South America accompanied by the phan-
tom of her heroic namesake.

Busy on the ancient sea-roads of the Mediterranean—and except for bare-ribbed little steamers packed with emigrants that crossed Admiral Christopher Columbus's "ocean sea" to Brazil and Argentina—Italy had no place in the myth of transatlantica until well into the twentieth century. But when the architects and designers of Florence, Trieste, and Genoa were ready to cut in, they did so with such misplaced confidence and bravura that, stylistically speaking, they all by themselves reintroduced the fedora and the toque into the era of the Homburg and the cloche.

This deferential bow to the recent past may have been comforting to the divas and *bassi profundi* who posed for photographs on deck. But passé magnificence from provincial designers was of little interest to maritime observers charged with chronicling the lives of ocean liners and anathema to those Italians for whom the aesthetic wave of Futurism had come to be the only one to ride. Consequently, the sudden entry of Italy into the higher realms of travel *di lusso* has been either ignored or translated into little more than shipyard statistics. But the remarkable fact is that, when the superliners of Great Britain, Germany, and France were coming out of oblivion and the backwaters of World War I, two little jewel-box liners from Genoa had begun to cut a swath and set a course toward Italian triumphs at sea entirely unanticipated. It would be fifteen years before what they initiated became clear. When it did, the Italian merchant marine was revealed as counting in its fleet the most fantastic examples of the ocean liner as a product of operatic *bella figura* and, at the same time, the most technologically advanced and decoratively avant-garde passenger vessels extant, including one flying the Blue Riband.

RISORGIMENTO SALOONS AND LIBERTY VERANDAHS — *LA FAMIGLIA* COPPEDÈ

Lotusland.

Carved, polychromed, carpeted, and tiled to within a hair's breadth of the lunatic, *Conte Russo*'s Smoking Room—"in Moorish style after the Alcazar in Seville"— boasted all the fittings of *gran lusso* transportation and then some. But it was 1924. The French were about to redefine the decorative arts in their Paris exposition and Germany was already on its way to a new aesthetic order at the Bauhaus in Weimar. The Italians, it seems, were content with yet another recycling of their own heritage.

Idiosyncratic in conception but painstakingly crafted and lavished with custom-made artworks (*right*, Carlo Coppedè's allegorical ceiling panel from the ship's library), the little *Conte* liners were sources of great pride to their homeport passengers and—aesthetics notwithstanding—brought Italy onto the Western ocean to stay.

Early in the twenties, Italy entered the transatlantic picture with two little liners—the *Conte Rosso* and the *Conte Verde*—dressed to the nines in the fashions of 1905. Built for Lloyd Sabaudo at Clydebank, they entered service—Genoa and Naples to New York—in 1922 and 1923, respectively, carrying huge complements of emigrants in squalor and one-eighth or one-ninth of their numbers in luxury. Unconcerned with the scramble for tourist boatloads by companies operating out of the English Channel, they catered almost exclusively to Italians. And what they offered natives was a peculiarly Italianate selection of historical debris from the same centuries-old warehouse from which Johannes Poppe had drawn the *putti* and damasks of the first instances of waterborne baroque.

Behind the *Conte*s was no individual designer but a dynasty, the family Coppedè. Florentines, Mariano and his sons Gino, Adolfo, and Carlo conducted business under the rubric La Casa Artistica, founded in 1885 and soon extended to include offices in Trieste and Genoa. Attuned to the tastes of a still highly visible old regime and to the often megalomaniac aspirations of an expanding *alta borghesia*, the Coppedès flourished from the start. Within a year of its founding, La Casa Artistica numbered among its clients J. Pierpont Morgan in London, the Rothschilds in Paris, the Marquesa de la Motilla in Seville, and, at home, members of the royal House of Savoy still rich and active enough to be concerned with domestic refurbishment. On the evidence of preserved photographs and *progetti*, it would appear that Mariano Coppedè gave his illustrious clients a choice of spurious historical imitations and doggedly literal reconstructions which, gathered into one place, would constitute a sort

Familiar Face.
A group of passengers headed for Genoa aboard *Conte Grande* in the late thirties are treated to an unexpected extra with their tour of the ship's bridge.

(Below) Conte Rosso and *Conte Verde* purposefully go their separate ways in a painting commissioned by Lloyd Sabaudo in 1921.

Filtered Daylight.
(Right) Light through tinted glass enhanced Carlo Coppedè's tapestries of medieval hunting scenes in the lightwell of *Conte Rosso*'s *Prima Classe* entrance foyer. Elsewhere, heavily worked oak and mahogany and the designer's apparent abhorrence of undecorated surface reveal a reverence for the Italianate. *(Above)* A *progetto* from *La Casa Artistica* detailing window and wall treatment for one of *Conte Rosso*'s salons. *(Entrance foyer illustration courtesy of Donato Riccesi, Trieste; detail courtesy of Mauro Cozzi, Florence)*

of post-Risorgimento Disneyland. To these, he and his sons added their own original attempts to extend the long history of fantastic architecture in Italy. Among the latter are Gino's complex of apartment houses and mansions in a part of Rome known today as the Quartiere Coppedè and, more prominently, Genoa's towering mud-pie folly, Castello Mackenzie, now owned by American Mitchell Wolfson, Jr.

Not far into the century, father and sons had already established a mode—*"monumentalmente coppedèiano"*—distinctive enough then, but destined to become a public joke, a joke having little or no impact on its perpetrators. The Coppedès continued to duplicate ancient history and on occasion, with less enthusiasm than opportunism, to appropriate touches of the new international spirit. Even when vulgarized to the point of farce, these were often effective in the boldness of the aesthetic banditry they disclosed.

Picture *Palazzo*.
In the late twenties, the devotion of the Coppedès to Tuscan Renaissance was expanded by an impulse toward eclecticism of the same sort that produced the Roxy rococo of the American movie palace. The ballroom of the *Conte Grande*—her Salone delle Feste—was one of its most extravagant expressions, literally (the room occupied the central part of three decks) and figuratively, in its mixture of Iberian Mauresque, Risorgimento balusters, and a burst of Oriental schmaltz unrestrained by a touch of Chippendale.

Completed a year after the *Conte Grande*'s maiden voyage in 1928, Genoa's Grand Hotel Colombia *(facing page)* had similar, if slightly more restrained, decor. ("Italia" Navigazione, Genoa; CIGA Hotels Archive, Milan)

The Coppedè influence on *arredo navale* (Italian for "ship decoration") would not be visible until 1908. Then, at the age of sixty-seven, Mariano was commissioned by Trieste's Lloyd Sabaudo to take charge of the interiors of the company's British-built *Principe di Udine*. This little bijou of a ship, of the same size as the first luxury liners from Germany, showed a lavish high hand that would find larger employment when Mariano was awarded a contract putting him and his sons in charge of the First Class accommodations of the *Conte Rosso* and *Conte Verde*. To hurry things along, the Coppedès sent their own woodworkers, ironworkers, and upholsterers to Clydebank. There, nearly two decades after the *Lusitania* had come into shape in the yards of John Brown, Ltd., the interiors of the new ships were painted, carved, and hung with swag in a manner which, already outmoded by 1905, had been consigned to the German phase of decorative aberration. Thus began the Coppedè dynasty's involvement with the operatic period of *palazzi flottanti* that would last until the arrival, in 1932, of the great *Conte di Savoia*.

With all the dignity of a miniature *Aquitania*, the *Conte Rosso* first took her pastiche of period styles across the Atlantic in March 1922. Iberian Mauresque in one room, she was Florentine *alla Vasari* and Pompeiian in others, with touches of Liberty (the Italian interpretation of Art Nouveau) and moments of embryonic Art Deco interspersed. Confidently Italian in spirit at a time when Italy had no clear signature at sea, she joined the requisitioned and rehabilitated ships of northern countries and, impervious to their overwhelming size and with no ambitions to break their speed records, began a maritime revival in which, moving from *fiorentino* fustian to *triestino* functionalism, Italian designers would put their indelible mark on the final years of the ocean-liner era.

Meanwhile, a succession of ever larger ships, as much alike in historical pretension and tentative modernism as to constitute an Italian genre, took to the sea-lanes. In effect, if not in intention, they confirmed and reconfirmed the hegemony of the Coppedès throughout the twenties. Small by northern standards, and never conceived as rivals, these liners brought to the North Atlantic a degree of showiness, even gaudiness, considered passé, especially by designers charged to bring old liners into conformity with plainer contemporary taste and to decorate new ones in the emergent idioms of Art Deco.

As even lay observers might then have suspected, and as historians have subsequently pointed out, a direct influence upon Italian ship interiors was the Hollywood epic as exemplified by Cecil B. De Mille, as well as the glitzy decor of imaginary nightclubs where movie gangsters cut their deals. Sometimes overdone to the point of hilarity, and as historically phony as the settings they attempted to anthologize, these liners—in the order of their launchings: *Conte Biancamano*, *Saturnia*, *Conte Grande*, *Vulcania*—nevertheless brought to transatlantica a degree of fantasy and unbridled hyperbole that would soon be forever muted.

Like *der Meister* Johannes Poppe, *i maestri* Coppedè lived to see the day when their collective skill in imitation, appropriation, and replication was grudgingly recognized by at least one younger designer of promise who, by nature and training, would be expected to admire none of it. As in Germany, where the ascendance of Bruno Paul and Rudolf Schröder had reduced the role of the aging Poppe to that of a marginal contributor to

Music Room.
(Facing page, far left) Winged figures of an operatic flamboyance flank the short staircase leading from *Conte Rosso*'s upper dining saloon into the ship's Music Room.

(Center) Stimulated by cavorting muses in a Pompeiian frieze, a soloist in swallowtail and his accompanist rehearse selections perhaps for the passenger show that usually took place on the last night of a voyage and was often the scene of bravado eclipsing talent.

(Above) Better than two decks high, the Sale da Pranzo aboard *Conte Rosso* and *Conte Verde* were unique at the time for their placement high in the ships' superstructures where, although more subject to sea motion, they offered the dual benefits of natural lighting and good ventilation. Rooms like these gave rise to the term *monumentalmente coppedèiano. (All three courtesy of Donato Riccesi, Trieste)*

operations he had earlier supervised with a commanding hand, so in Italy was the family Coppedè forced to accommodate the rising star of Gustavo Pulitzer Finali and the new conceptions of *arredo navale* he was about to introduce.

Eventually, the Coppedès had to bow out. They did so with a characteristic brio resonant enough to remind generations to come that, when they disappeared behind the studio-lot façades of Egypt, Rome, and Granada from which they had emerged, so did the last brave representations of history-as-fantasy on the oceans. Adolfo was the one chosen to make this valedictory gesture, and he carried it off by producing one of the most famous shipboard spaces of the century. This was the Galleria Colonna of the *Conte di Savoia*. Like a last, Parthian shot from the retreating forces of a superannuated tradition, Adolfo's *galleria*, reconstructed with archaeological fidelity, was the primary social center of a ship otherwise conceived as the ultimate expression of modernism afloat. Recidivist in intention, unapologetically imperial in detail, this room was one of the last decorative statements of a vanishing day when the first purpose of marine designers was to keep the sea out of sight, out of sound, and out of mind. For a few short years, the Galleria Colonna cosseted passengers in its antique opulence, then sank to the bottom of the Adriatic off Capodistria, a victim of British bombers that successfully targeted the *Conte di Savoia* and so brought to an end the first great phase of Italian liners with an explosive finality which, as time would tell, made an even more illustrious phase inevitable.

Liberty of London.
The lady's scarf very likely comes from the Regent Street emporium, and the gentleman in the steamer cap seems no stranger to *la moda inglese*. Their setting, co-opting Egyptian lotus capitals, pharaonic masks, and fine-mesh wicker furniture Americans would eventually call "early Taft," is a throwback to the brief period of Art Nouveau, which Italians interpreted rather broadly and called by the name "Liberty," after the English firm's renowned textile patterns.

THE SISTERS FROM TRIESTE—
SATURNIA AND *VULCANIA*

Starting Point.
1927—the *Saturnia* of Cosulich Lines, a floating anthology of taste new and old, good and bad, Risorgimento and Irredenta, prepares for her long maiden voyage from Trieste, down the Adriatic, through the Mediterranean to Gibraltar and out across the Atlantic to South America. Surviving changing tastes and World War II, *Saturnia* and her sister sailed into a new era that would see *servizio di lusso italiano* take its place with the most highly regarded forms of transatlantic accommodation.

Verandah Suite.
(Facing page) Sometimes unusable in the Mediterranean, seldom on the Atlantic, summery little balconies with wicker tables and chairs were a pleasant feature and strong selling point of *di lusso* quarters on both the *Vulcania* and *Saturnia*. A desirable amenity in warm waters, the private verandah would, in future years, become a high-status commonplace on ships built exclusively for pleasure cruising.

Among ships of an older dispensation still in service as recently as thirty years ago, few are remembered with more tender affection than the *Saturnia* and *Vulcania*. Except for one concession to modernism—enormous single, squat funnels that made them identifiable at a glance—they were otherwise uncompromised examples of the antique somehow never relegated to the passé. Decorated largely by the family Coppedè, they were subject to its terms; once more, the labeled baggage of the past was moved piecemeal onto the wide decks of the present. What the Coppedès sent to sea from the yards of the Cantiere Navale Triestino was so absurdly grandiose, so confidently wrongheaded, and so hopelessly charming that questions of outmoded fashion and contemporary relevance were never asked.

Two of the four Italian passenger liners to survive World War II (the others were the *Conte Grande* and the *Conte Biancamano*), these Cosulich Line sisters went into service four and seven years before the *Rex* and the *Conte di Savoia*, then became their running mates. Sharing the same ocean routes, they seemed indifferent to the reputations of the larger ships for Blue Riband speed and Mussolini exhibitionism and, in their own prosperity, survived to teach the postwar world what the liner conceived as a historical anecdote was all about.

With their introduction of private outdoor verandahs, the *Saturnia* and *Vulcania* became modest forerunners of a new out-of-doors idea of seagoing. Indoors, their radiant glass domes, marble halls, and opera-box fittings perpetuated a defunct palatial order. Grandly obsolescent, they hung on long enough to witness the demise of La Casa Artistica and the beginnings of a confluence of Italian ingenuity, taste, and flair which, in the years immediately after World War II, made Milan the fountainhead of contemporary design on the Continent.

Unlike their *Conte* predecessors, the *Saturnia* and *Vulcania* carried the imprint of hands other than those of the Coppedès—some with much the same itch to make configurations of everything in sight, some with a softer touch and a feel for flat surfaces and unadorned verticals then changing the look of ships almost everywhere but in Italy. The most typically Coppedèian contribution to the *Saturnia* was a ballroom the likes of which had not been seen since the "meringue baroque" of Johannes Poppe's dining hall in the *Kaiser Wilhelm der Grosse* of 1897. However, as if to prove that historical eclecticism could be comparatively low-key and selective, the firm of Marsh, Jones and Cribb, from Leeds, and the firm of Partois & Fix, from Vienna, were given opportunity to modify Coppedèian excess in rooms appointed with a delicacy that honored period pieces without magnifying their character or nudging them into parody.

Austrian artisans of every stripe were no strangers to Trieste, but a team of decorators from as far away as

Final Outburst.
Indifferent to new decorative ideas flaring
up like brushfires all around them, the
Coppedès, remaining within their own
preserve, designed identical *sale delle feste*
(facing page) for the *Saturnia* and *Vul-*
cania, nominally in the style of Louis XIV,
but unmatched in flourishes of meringue
baroque since the heyday of Johannes
Poppe. Elsewhere on board, designers
from England, Austria, and the homeport
of Trieste brought a palliative touch to the
sister ships with less strident period settings like the delicate, blue-lacquered
cineserie of the *sala di scrittura* at right.
(Both courtesy of Donato Riccesi, Trieste)

the north of England suggested a welcome breach in Italian parochialism. The even more surprising contributor to the new ships was Gustavo Pulitzer Finali, the hometown architect and designer already known for avant-garde notions he'd picked up in travels abroad and a philosophy of ship decoration widely at odds with prevailing thought. On his way to becoming the leading theorist of *arredo navale* over many years to come, Pulitzer Finali entered, so to speak, by a side door.

Given the aesthetic temper of the times and assuming the kinds of in-house rivalry that would inevitably attend a project as important as the building of the two greatest passenger ships of Italy, his participation evokes questions. Was his acceptance of Coppedèian hyperbole a clue to unadmitted respect? Or was it a kind of canny dissemblance essential to the terms of his employment? Whatever, his starboard *galleria*, or "Solemn Room"—a sort of retreat, half chapel, half study—was an exercise in sacerdotal kitsch so faithful to Coppedèian ideals as to amount to an act of reverence, or of cynical traducement. Stuffed with the swag of countries bordering the Mediterranean from Morocco to Turkey, it included even samples of the graffiti left behind by the several waves of Crusaders.

As if to compensate for this apparently pusillanimous bow to his colleagues, Pulitzer Finali then went on to

Frieze.
From the Acropolis via the British Museum, a domesticated version of the Parthenon's pedimental ornamentation is interpolated into a Greco-Roman setting for *Saturnia*'s First Class Dining Saloon *(right)*. Conceived and executed by the English firm of Marsh, Jones and Cribb, the room's personality—as indeed, that of the entire ship—seemed split between a fondness for the burnished rubble of the past and a flirtation with the sleek minimalism of the future.

No such discrepancy is apparent, however, in *La Casa Artistica*'s congenial Grill Room *(above)*. "Decorated in the style of the joyful fifteenth century in Tuscany," the cozy room was a Promenade Deck diversion and a mealtime alternative to *Saturnia*'s sacerdotal dining room. *(Both courtesy of Donato Riccesi, Trieste)*

give the *Saturnia* a Smoking Room remarkable enough to redeem his promise without overstepping the conservative line. An unexpectedly harmonious mixture of Marco Polo *cineserie* and St. Jamesian plush and leather, this room featured daylight—floods of it through tall side windows and from a vaulted ceiling composed of squares of paned glass. Airy and colorful, it conspicuously lacked the masculine, denlike appurtenances of other rooms of the type, except for an anomaly. One high section of wall under the skylight was devoted to game-hunters' trophies—row upon row of the little antlered and horned heads of elands, impalas, and wildebeests.

Nevertheless, the *Saturnia* and *Vulcania* belong to the Coppedès, Gino and Carlo, approaching a time in their professional lives when they were motivated less toward whimsical reinterpretations of history than toward reproductions of it. Variation, adaptation, and other uses of an established genre are open to judgment in regard to their local application. Reproduction, on the other hand, is relatively safe. Choosing it, the Coppedès were in the clear. Critics who found their pretensions farcical and, as an example, might want to make comic capital of their swimming pool on the *Vulcania* would not have the brothers themselves to contend with, but the mummified ashes of the architects of Pompeii.

132

Tactical Retreats.
A man who would become famous as the first Italian designer of ship interiors with a functionalist aesthetic, Gustavo Pulitzer Finali was not, in his early years, incapable of concocting period reproductions as required. His apparent capitulation to prevailing taste in the *Saturnia*'s fustian Solemn Room *(right)* was exception more than rule, however. Elsewhere, his early work evidences an adroitness in choosing those period styles which best lent themselves to modernist treatment, as with the crisp Tudor of *Saturnia*'s Smoking Room *(above)*, and later in the choice of a minimal oriental screen motif for *Conte Grande*'s indoor pool. *(Both courtesy of Donato Riccesi, Trieste)*

"This," said a devotee of *Roma rediviva*, "is one of the most astonishing reconstructions they have ever attempted. . . . Not the austere antiquity of the handbook, but the opulence of Roman life at the height of imperial splendor. It is a vision of the luxurious fantasy of the Coppedès. Here we do not have influences but the full embodiment; not surrogation but authentication—bronzes, marbles, alabaster, encrustations of semi-precious stones, mosaics. Under the skylight, one descends small ledges of marble into a huge pool surrounded by columns and grotesque representations of Atlas on golden pediments."

The abstractive reductions and skimpy detailings of modernism could wait. Once more, and despite the death of Gino in 1927, the Coppedè dynasty had prevailed. Retractive in one decade, projective in another, the lens of history will ultimately reveal all that maritime historians may want to know of the contribution of the Coppedè to transatlantica. While assessment may be delayed, it is not too early to record a growing sentiment expressed in a phrase of the poet Elizabeth Bishop—"awful but cheerful."

From Pompeii to the Lido.
Indoor and outdoor swimming pools gave
Saturnia and *Vulcania* passengers a choice
of sun and shorts, or tank suits and an
unstinting ambience of marble and mosaic.
Dissatisfied with one, they could take the
first convenient elevator to the other.

Almost from the first, swimming pools
installed in ships were meant to evoke
Roman hygienic splendor, the motifs of
which were considered the only appropriate decorative style until modernism made
its way to sea. *(Courtesy of Donato Riccesi,
Trieste)*

Sunshine.
A poster by Dudovitch emphasizes the *sportivo* aspects of a Southern Route crossing.

(Above right) Touted by Cosulich as an innovation, the upper-deck accommodation with private verandah would quickly become a standard feature of the most luxurious transatlantic liners.

Comparatively rare in ships of other nations, above-the-bow, forward-facing verandahs like this one on *Vulcania* were more the norm on Italian liners plying the sunnier Southern Route to the Mediterranean. Therapeutic solariums by day, they had to be shuttered or otherwise blacked out by night in order not to interfere with navigation from the bridge, usually directly above. (All three courtesy of Donato Riccesi, Trieste)

135

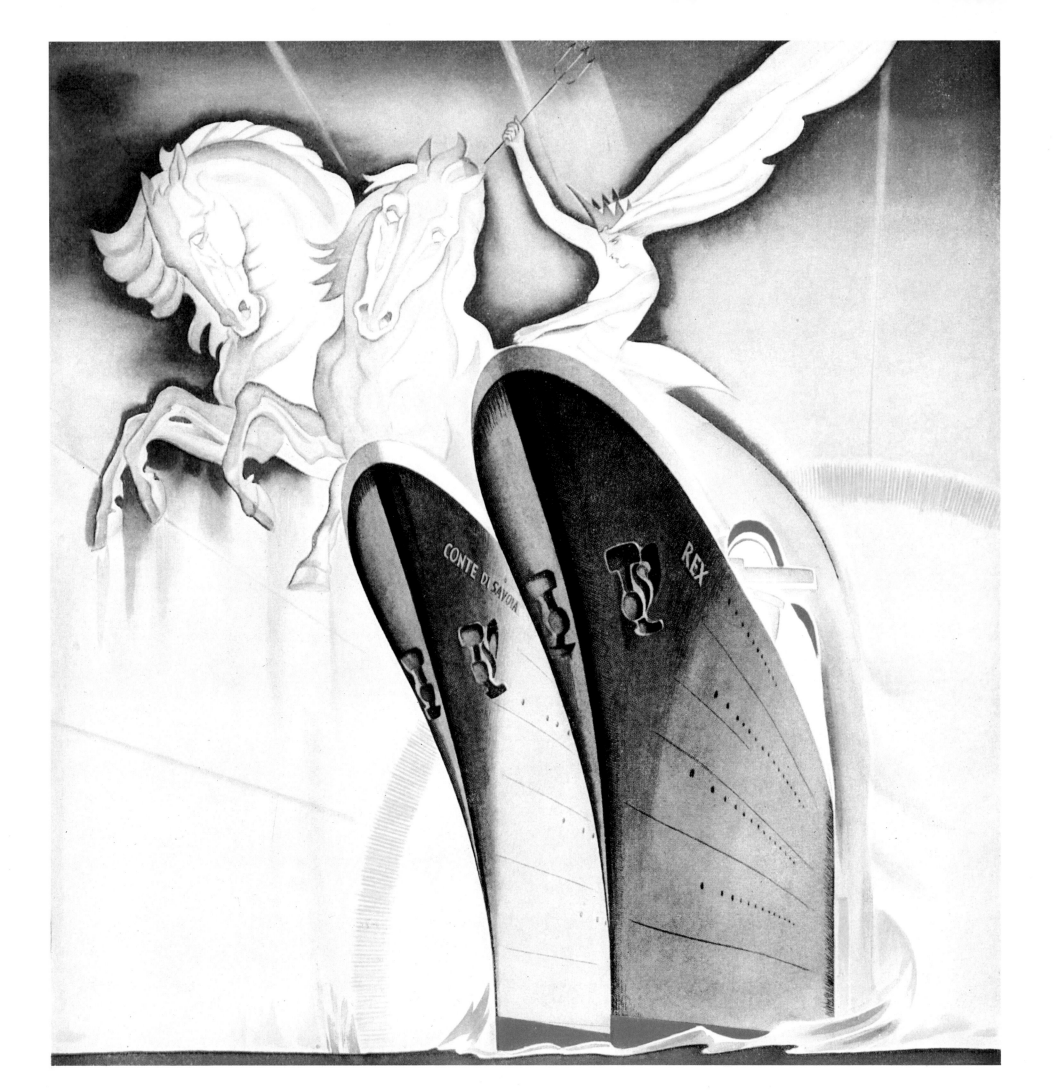

PART SIX

Transatlantic Style, Transatlantic Dash: Liners of the Golden Age

―――――――――――――

Emissaries.
Apparently under the protection of Amphi-
trite, wife of Poseidon, the shining new
liners *Rex* and *Conte di Savoia* make their
maiden way across the Atlantic. The illustration is from a September 1932 advertisement heralding the near-simultaneous
commissioning of Fascist Italy's newest
achievements.

By the middle thirties, the ocean liner as a species had come into its majority and full estate. Nothing launched after those years would ever be bigger or faster (save for the *United States* which, in 1952, was capable of crossing from New York to Southampton in seventy-two hours), and nothing would add to or subtract from the already full-blown legend of a business transformed into a romance.

In the dazzling yet moribund international fleet that hard times would decimate and airborne bombs would destroy, all that the great ships of the early century were, or would become, was handsomely in evidence. *Belle-époque* opulence and its Art Deco sequel still lured travelers onto the *Paris* and the *Ile de France*. The "shippiness" long sought by designers bent on uniting form and function had finally been achieved in the steel-and-chrome sleekness of the *Bremen* and the *Conte di Savoia*. The passé but beloved ambience of "White Star Roman" still characterized the dowager *Olympic* and the *Majestic*. And the newly appreciated embellishments of its counterpart, "*Berengaria* baroque," could still be enjoyed on the ship bearing that name as well as on her running mates, the classic *Mauretania* and the once peerless *Aquitania*. Laden with the century's transitory styles and its exquisite examples of handcrafted wood, metal, and glass, each of these paragons would soon be replaced by ships surrendered to plastics, modules, stainless steel, and all the other temporalities of mass production. Meanwhile, the last swaths and tassels of the Risorgimento continued to festoon the *Vulcania* and *Saturnia*. The white vision of the *Empress of Britain* still floated beneath the bluffs of the Château Frontenac. Then, like leviathans wandering into the shallows of maritime history, along came the *Normandie* and the *Queen Mary*, soon joined by the *Queen Elizabeth*. This trio, in one audacious leap, carried the era of the sumptuous into the realm of the unsurpassable.

137

DIE OZEAN-EXPRESS—
BREMEN AND EUROPA

Streamlines.
Eclipsed in 1913 by Hapag's *Imperator* and then losing their 34,000-ton *Columbus* at Versailles, Norddeutscher Lloyd reassumed supremacy on the Atlantic with two ships of overwhelming power and a distinctive, blunt-funneled silhouette that quietly proclaimed the future. On July 16, 1929, the 52,000-ton, 938-foot-long *Bremen* dashed for New York at 27.83 knots, capturing the coveted Blue Riband and inaugurating "*Die Ozean-Express*."

Late Afternoon.
George Grosz's acid is absent from this parody in a 1932 *Fortune* article on the *Bremen*, but the artist, Zdzislaw Czermanski, nonetheless manages to convey the discrepancy between the lumpish self-satisfaction of the ship's First Class passengers and the audacious new conveyance carrying them across the ocean in just five days. (*Zdzislaw Czermanski painting courtesy of Time Life, Inc.*)

By the mid-twenties, Germany was back in the transatlantic business with several modest-sized and nondescript ships and one handsome, comfortable, "democratized" liner that showed herself a winner. Launched in 1922, Norddeutscher Lloyd's *Columbus* was one of the first liners to be built with an eye to the new class distribution determined by the loss of emigrant revenue. Her interiors were a compendium of domestic architectural references going clear back to Johannes Poppe, but she would prove to be the last Norddeutscher Lloyd liner to employ a purely traditional decorative vocabulary. Encouraged by the fact that, in 1926, she carried almost as many passengers to and from Bremen, New York, and the several Channel ports as did the flagships of her British and French competitors, her owners decided that it was time to make the boldest German bid for supremacy since the heyday of Albert Ballin and Charles Mewès.

As they devised plans for the *Bremen* and *Europa*, these men were motivated, first, to make "emphatic pronunciations of the principle of rapid speed," then to produce tonnage equal to but, curiously enough, no greater than that of Germany's legendary prewar liners. Finally, they wanted a kind of interior decoration that would do away with the Wagnerian emblazonry and overstuffed castle-on-the-Rhine pretensions of a bygone era and—bold, bare, and shiny—emulate in a German way *le style paquebot* of the newborn *Ile de France* and so follow her into the twentieth century. Toward this end they enlisted the services of Fritz August Breuhaus de Groot, a versatile architect from Düsseldorf with a mission as clear as his monocle.

"The ostentatious luxury of former times," said Breuhaus de Groot, "which no longer appeals to the man of today, has been avoided in the interior decorations by laying stress on the purity of form, on the beauty of line and on the superior quality of the material. The architecture of the *Bremen* emancipates us from a time which is not our own and leads us into the grandeur of the present age, in which we desire to breathe and not to suffocate."

His statement echoed those of other designers for whom decorative replication of historical periods had led to one good thing: by 1925 or so, the past had been unloaded—Louis by French Louis, Chippendale by Sheraton, *cineseria fiorentina* by Iberian Mauresque—onto the decks of a dozen old-school liners still plying the Atlantic. Advanced technology, long taken for granted or obscured by the visible fancies of decorators who did their work in ateliers and not in shipyards, would at last have its day. New conceptions of arts and crafts, reflecting the reductive beauty of Constantin Brancusi, Antoine Pevsner, Naum Gabo, would equate the antique with the obsolescent or the moribund. In France, Le Corbusier had already articulated what Breuhaus de Groot was about: "The ship is the first stage in the realization of a world organized according to the new spirit." This

Alpine Golfers.
Devotees of fashionable sports were woven into tapestries hung at the corners of *Bremen*'s lofty but informal main dining room. Above the unceremonious entrance, a transverse corridor opened into the room and provided a location for members of the ship's orchestra to present musical diversions at mealtime. (*Both courtesy of Erika Lisson, Hapag-Lloyd Archive, Bremen*)

was the spirit in which a modern aesthetic would be defined by builders with a sense of the splendor of machines, by architects unhampered by the maniacal eclecticism of decorators.

The keel of the *Bremen* was laid in the Weser shipyards of her namesake city on June 18, 1927, at the same time that the keel of her sister ship was laid in the Blohm & Voss yards of Hamburg. On consecutive days in August 1928, before spectators in the scores of thousands and a press corps that numbered in the hundreds, the *Europa* and *Bremen* slid down their respective ways. This joint launching of more than 100,000 tons of German shipbuilding made a splash reported in newspapers around the world, and at home was heard by a vast radio audience tuned in to cheer the return of the fatherland to its "rightful" place on the ocean. This star-turn sister act might have gained even greater coverage had plans for simultaneous record-breaking maiden voyages been fulfilled. But the *Europa* suffered serious damage by fire while being fitted out and had to hang back for all of a year before she was able to join her running mate.

At no more than a glance, the *Bremen* afloat communicated the excitement of something arrestingly new, overwhelmingly powerful, and genuinely novel. Lines of a hull constructed on an elongated oval plan gave her a staunch look of energy-in-reserve; the bulbous foot that ballooned out from her bow was the first ever to replace the conventional cutwater on a ship of her size; and her two massive buff funnels, pear-shaped and squat, did away with the precarious stovepipe feeling that the wire-supported stacks of prewar liners inevitably produced. Her two masts were uncommonly short and, like the funnels, raked back with a military smartness. A bold

The Return of the Rhine Maidens.
(Above) Prefiguring Esther Williams and
the water ballets of MGM by nearly twenty
years, Germanic nymphs entertained passengers on the *Bremen* with bare-breasted
good humor and a generally liberated
outlook. This was the level of artworks
placed throughout a ship so technologically in advance of her time that she
"gleamed like a new planet."

Dining High.
Equivalent in exclusiveness to the Verandah Grills and Ritz Carlton restaurants of
other ships, the *Bremen's* Sun Deck Restaurant *(right)* was available to First Class
passengers, as advertisements put it, "by
special allowance." Designed by Norddeutscher Lloyd's old hand, Paul Hoffman,
according to traditional ideas of scale, it
nevertheless echoed the streamlined aesthetic evident elsewhere on board in its
repetition of the ship's signature arc and
circle motifs.

suggestion of streamlining emanated from her rounded-off bridge; and, at 102 feet, her beam was the broadest on
the Atlantic. All in all, her builders had achieved what they envisioned—"a vast seagoing cathedral of steel."

The most adventurous thing about the *Bremen*, however, was the fact that her builders had put aside the
notion of an ocean liner as a grand hotel with engines in favor of an approach in which a ship's intrinsic volume
and shape were regarded not as limitations to be overcome but as opportunities to be exploited. For the first time
since the *Vaterland* of 1913, these builders had provided decorators with a superstructure opened through by
divided funnel uptakes and the unimpeded use of stem-to-stern space these made possible. Responding to the
advantage, designers took care to feel out the lines of structure and, as a principle, to show how interiors might
conform to the closures and curves these lines dictated. The particular motif that gave character to the *Bremen's*
grand saloon—a series of elongated and arched windows open to daylight—was repeated with variations
throughout the ship, sometimes in arcs of gleaming brass, at other times in circularities ranging from stabile
objects to structural domes. Consequently, the *Bremen* achieved an overall "shippiness" that ran directly counter
to the cozy Cotswold-cottage air of British ships, the picture-palace schmaltz of those from Italy, and the bland
Statler-lobby atmosphere of ships out of New York.

Yet . . . and yet. In avoiding the "ostentatious luxury of former times," the decorators of the *Bremen* came
to pitfalls rendering all claim to "the grandeur of the present age" spurious. Replacing the overstuffed with the
understated, they came up with interiors as forbiddingly clinical as emergency wards. The vaunted economy of

Thematic Circularity.
Conceived in fluid curves and sleek surfaces, *Bremen*'s Festhalle *(this page, below)* featured a centrally placed fountain of light that matched an electric pattern of hues to the changing moods of the dance music. Ahead of its time in streamline effects, *Bremen*'s ballroom, like much of the rest of the ship, was "modernistic" but not seminal.

Crossroads.
(This page, above) Designed in the same year as two icons of the International Style—Mies van der Rohe's Barcelona Pavilion and Le Corbusier's Villa Savoye—Fritz August Breuhaus de Groot's *Bremen* and *Europa* bear the stamp of a different aesthetic, what has been variously referred to as "Fascist Modern" or "The Monumental Style." Characterized by attenuated forms and exaggerated scale but retaining classical notions of symmetry, it was a style more evolutionary than revolutionary.

The transverse cutaway rendering of the *Bremen*'s main stairwell *(facing page)*, prescribing the decorative treatment for each landing from the C-Deck *speisesaal* entrance at bottom to the terraced vestibule of the Sonnendeck Restaurant at top, foreshadows the work of Roger-Henri Expert on the *Normandie* and Albert Speer in the Reichstag, and suggests Breuhaus de Groot's predisposition to Beaux Arts convention over Bauhaus radicalism.

means by which they meant to make passengers more conscious of the ship's matchless power than of luxury was a concept both daring and advanced; but it was also premature. Historicism as an inspiration for the interior decorator was over with; the demand for comfort in beguiling surroundings was not. It soon became apparent that the unprecedented functionalism of a ship that "gleamed like a new planet" was attained at the cost of almost everything that had made the meanings of the term *gemütlich* a German distinction and a German preserve.

True to her technological promise, the *Bremen* entered service with maiden voyages on which, going and coming, she broke all existing records. By this time, Bauhaus as a cultural phenomenon and as an institution had been prominently in existence for ten years. The conjunction is important, if only as an indication of why, beyond her mechanical eminence, the new supership could not bear scrutiny.

The instant success of the group of pioneer designers gathered in Weimar had made it thrillingly and abundantly clear that the twentieth century had found a working vocabulary of unlimited imagination and practical aesthetics and that its accent was German. In a way that was unprecedented in modern history, the influence of Bauhaus around the world was already pervasive enough to have supplied blueprints for the houses people would live in, the shapes of the chairs they would sit on, the paintings they would look at, even the posters that would invite them to take part in a vision of life based on newly revealed harmonies of color, volume, and line teased into being by ingenuity pursuing the feasible. Dismissing out of hand the thousand gifts of Bauhaus which enchanted the rest of the world, the decorators of the *Bremen* proceeded in the confidence of ignorance—or in that spirit of self-preservation best described as "the revenge of the small cabinetmakers"—to turn the great ship into a seaborne showcase of tawdriness.

Were there a catalogue raisonné to document what was on exhibition aboard the *Bremen*, it would feature tapestries of American Indians in the snow tending pots on tripods made of sticks; sturdy lady golfers in cloche hats and tweed skirts, teeing off in Alpine settings; doomed boars surrounded by oafish hunters and ravenous dogs; stained-glass windows depicting animals as obstreperous noise-makers (a graphic gesture honoring one of the myths of the city of Bremen); murals in which country bumpkins in the costumes of the twenties perform the rites of spring and fall; bare-breasted Rhine maidens in the image of Esther Williams disporting for the pleasure of voyeurist elves in buskins.

Tapestries and wall paintings on the level of gas-station–calendar art may have confounded the otherwise refreshing pretensions of the *Bremen*. But some of her most publicized features were even more depressing. In the center of the dance floor—where, according to the English version of the ship's entertainment program, "Dancing with little surprises will enjoy the guests"—stood a fountain somehow constructed of layers of kitchen utensils, including one of translucent glass through which glowed a changing spectrum of pastel light. The walls of the Writing Room were paneled with tall tablets enscrolled with homiletic advice from famous contributors to American folk wisdom, among them Ella Wheeler Wilcox: "*Lach,*" and the world laughs with you; "*wein, und du weinst allein.*"

August 25, 1939.
(Above) The last Sunday luncheon menu the *Bremen* would ever print. In New York three days later, she was detained to allow United States government agents to search her thoroughly for spies and ammunition, then allowed to slide away, so the story goes, without one passenger to witness her crew lined up on deck to give a valedictory Nazi salute to the Statue of Liberty. Her long voyage home—via Soviet Murmansk, then down the east coast of Norway—took four months and was her last. She burned at her Bremerhaven dock fifteen months later . . . whether out of carelessness or by sabotage has never been determined.

(Right) A menu cover from a few years earlier. *(Mark D. Warren Collection)*

Modern *Schwimbad.*
Drawing its only warmth from a miniature bar and the conviviality of its tank-suited clientele, *Bremen*'s pool was the very model of cool modernism and probably *Architekt* Breuhaus de Groot's clearest reference—intentional or not—to the emergent International Style. *(Hapag-Lloyd Archive, Bremen)*

The First Class Shooting Gallery, on the other hand, was inventive and new: between its stockade walls was a movie screen across which flew, leaped, or crawled creatures which, once "hit," were stopped in their tracks to allow the marksman to confirm just which breast, limb, or wing his imaginary bullet had severed.

Not since the *Great Eastern* of the middle nineteenth century had the Atlantic Ocean countenanced anomaly on so vast a scale. A superlative mechanism with a pavilion sweep of public rooms, the *Bremen* was lavish with space and almost nothing else. Instead of uniting the newly appreciated beauty of technological ingenuity with that branch of German genius which had defined the modern for decades to come, those responsible for the *Bremen* somehow contrived to unite awesomeness with inanity. Bypassing Bauhaus, and every other manifestation of emergent modernism, they reached into the vast warehouse of German kitsch and picked out all the doodaddery and cuteness that would serve to degrade what they were commissioned to enhance. The result was schizophrenia made visible . . . in all parts of the ship except those in which an all but forgotten decorator of genius was allowed to play his hand.

145

Like *Leviathan* and *Ile de France* before
them, *Bremen* and *Europa* were equipped
with catapults to launch planes carrying
mail. Up against the new *Graf Zeppelin*
which, beginning in 1928, routinely provided two-and-a-half-day transatlantic mail
service, the air/sea hybrid operated by
Norddeutscher Lloyd was not very strong
competition, but in 1929 it was technologically glamorous, attention-getting, and—
for passengers gathered for the event
outside the Sonnendeck Restaurant of
either express liner—wonderfully noisy
and exciting. While still twenty-four hours
from port, *Bremen* and *Europa* would hurl
their adopted Junkers W-34 float planes
into the wild blue and, three hours later, a
heavy bag of *Luftpost* would be handed
over to postal authorities on shore. For all
its drama, it was a costly operation—a
boon mainly for stamp collectors—and the
project was quietly suspended with the
onset of worldwide depression.

By all odds, and a twist of irony, the most engaging rooms on the *Bremen* were those executed by Rudolf
Schröder. His great years of Jugendstil *an Bord*, particularly as represented by the *George Washington* of 1909,
had never been matched in Art Nouveau delicacy; and he had been one of the first designers to favor the
coherent over the eclectic. Now, a full twenty years later, his First Class Smoking Room and Second Class Dining
Room demonstrated how the light touch of an obsolescent mode might be the saving grace of a ship stridently
new and with no pretense to charm.

Schröder's Smoking Room had a kind of miniature grandeur, with Mackintoshian chairs and tables giving a
now historical distinction to rotunda space enclosed by wood paneling and broken vertically by pillars veneered
with burl. In the Second Class Dining Room, he found ways to modify the insistent geometry of the *Bremen*'s
chrome-plated ancillas and their metallic gloss. Railings connecting the steps of a double staircase that led to a

Form Follows Function.
Or life imitates art. Finally, in the silhouettes of *Bremen* and *Europa*, the dream
imagery of great express liners cleaving
the waves—imagery devised by commercial illustrators during the twenties to
convey stylized notions of modernism,
speed, and efficiency—merged with reality. The new German ships were strikingly
advanced in appearance with long, clean
lines, flattened funnels, and raked masts.
But their wider-than-high stacks were so
abbreviated that their very function was all
but compromised. As a result, the ships'
rakish profiles were short-lived; by 1930
both *Bremen* and *Europa* had had their
uptakes raised to a more conventional
height and—in the process—their personalities modified to the merely imposing.
(Courtesy of Ted and Joan Hindmarsh)

pocket-size winter garden were done in irregular fretwork and painted white. Then, as if on a dare, he introduced a note of whimsy with a bow-front *balcone piccolo* for dinnertime concerts during which only the faces of string quartets were visible.

Anomaly itself: the steel caverns of the *Bremen* cradled some of the last hopes of that period of German aesthetic enlightenment spanning the years between the opening of Henri van de Velde's Folkwang Museum in Hagen up to the establishment of Bauhaus in Weimar. Had what these hopes promised been given more than a marginal role in the fitting-out of the great liner, a unifying harmony of the technical and the decorative might have transformed the *Bremen* from a ship without heart to a ship without peer.

THE EMPRESS FROM CANADA

Royalty.
Built on the Clydebank, christened in deference to the mother country, grand and white, the *Empress of Britain* was Canadian Pacific's largest passenger ship. Her career, thwarted by the Depression and terminated by World War II, was brief and tragic, but her glistening image is indelible, and the high standards of her offering on the North Atlantic assure her place on the lists of the greatest liners ever built. *(Facing page)* An artist's impression of an *Empress* suite. *(Both, Canadian Pacific Archives, Montreal)*

A dream without sequel, the *Empress of Britain* continues to haunt the imaginations of those for whom the ocean liner is a phenomenon greater than the sum of its parts, more than an inventory of its trappings; not a thing but a being.

Her brief life, begun in the Great Depression, lasted only until the early days of World War II. All but totally obscured by the worldwide attention given to the superliners that followed closely in her wake, she was the largest and most handsomely appointed ship to come from the British isles in nearly twenty years. The *Empress of Britain* slid down the ways of John Brown's Clydeside yards in June 1930 and, snow-white in the sun, made her maiden voyage from Southampton to Québec one year later.

At 42,000 tons plus, almost as big as the *Titanic*, she was the first ship of her size specifically designed to fulfill a dual purpose: northern-route crossings in the summer and—in the winter months when Montréal was ice-locked—around-the-world cruising. Consequently, illustrations of this most photogenic of ships are more apt to show her attended by sampans, outriggers, and bumboats than by the feisty tugs and sturdy tenders of the Temperate Zone. Yet the *Empress of Britain* was a true Atlantic liner in the great tradition. Overnight she turned the workaday lanes of Canada's St. Lawrence route to Europe into a passage stylish enough for anyone. She took her most affluent passengers across the ocean in five-room apartments with furnished balconies on the sea that could actually be used; others in spacious cabins offering a higher ratio of crew-to-passenger service than any of her contemporaries save the *Normandie*.

Observed from any distance, the *Empress* was a picture of serenity and grace. Cutting through the sparkling icefields of the Strait of Belle Isle or weaving her way through the magenta and orange fishing fleets of the Gates of Hercules, she personified power and gleamed like a white city. Her three buff funnels, robust yet dignified, made her one of the last of a breed of three-stackers that would otherwise include only the *Normandie* and the *Queen Mary*. Inside, she was a showcase for an extraordinary team of designers and decorators—Sir Frank William Brangwyn, Sir John Lavery, Sir Charles Allom, Edmund Dulac—whose individual efforts combined charm with daring in a series of public rooms, everywhere punctuated by Canadian motifs, that won her the reputation of being the most congenial and perhaps the most comfortable ship on the Atlantic.

Her Cathay Lounge—an audacious fantasy worked out in lipstick and ebony—reminded passengers that they were sailing under the house flag of the Canadian *Pacific* and of those years when other *Empress*es with clipper bows and racy lines were the most dependable connection between Vancouver and the Orient. Her Tennis Café, an airy conservatory with trellised walls and furnished in wicker, was an adjunct to the only full-size regulation tennis court on the high seas.

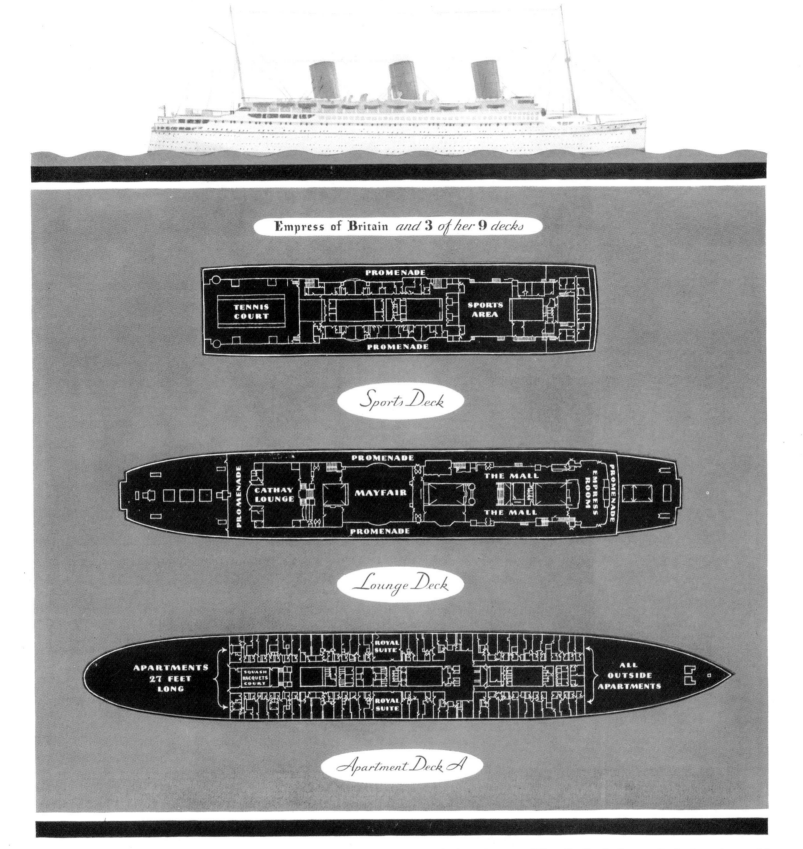

Empress of Britain *and* 3 *of her* 9 *decks*

Sports Deck

Lounge Deck

Apartment Deck A

ON THE SUN DECK, *you start your tan. On the Sports Deck, you play real tennis or look on from court-side café. On the Lounge Deck, devoted to social amusements, you dance, play bridge, read, or chat in a series of brilliant metropolitan club-rooms designed by Sir John Lavery {Empress Room}, Sir Charles Allom {Mayfair}, Edmund Dulac {Cathay Lounge}, Heath Robinson {Knickerbocker Bar} . . . or join the strollers on the long Mall. For the squash-racquets court, the gymnasium, and the Olympian Pool and café you descend to other decks . . . and you dine in the Salle Jacques Cartier under Frank Brangwyn's magnificent murals of plenty.*

Empress of Britain

5 DAYS TO EUROPE

Resort.
Promotional advertising free from the "expedient exaggeration" was as unusual in the thirties as it is today, but Canadian Pacific's representation of the generous proportions of its First Class accommodation was that rare exception. With cabins—referred to as apartments—averaging 325 square feet and all the amenities of a good suburban club, the *Empress* was more profligate of space than any luxury liner of her time and, consequently, admirably equipped to deliver on her promise.

Typecasting.
A Deanna Durbin look-alike in a well-dressed setting demonstrates rather convincingly the substantial comforts available to an *Empress* traveler—including that standard emblem of Hollywood fantasy, a white telephone. *(Canadian Pacific Archives, Montreal)*

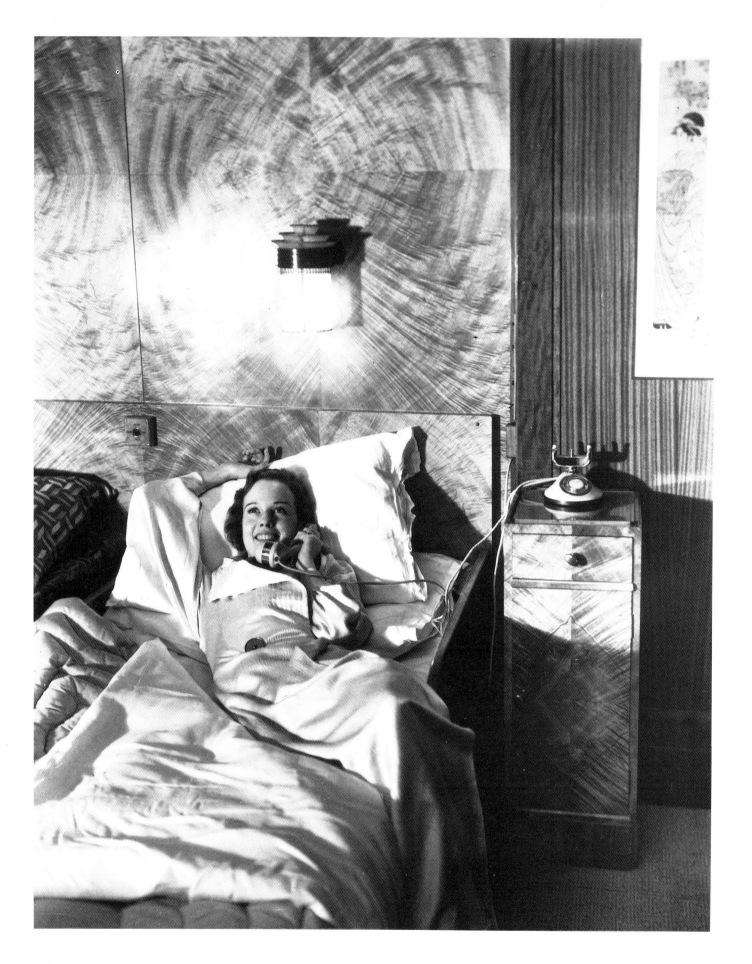

Ship Space.
A mirrored *Empress* ballroom big enough for Viennese waltzes and a Mayfair Lounge *(facing page)* of unusually sumptuous appointment and broad dimension reflect the concern of the *Empress of Britain*'s designers and sponsors for unprecedented breathing space, elbow room, and, not incidentally, retention of historical styles even in the face of encroaching modernism. *(Below)* Passengers gather for an evening's entertainment on "The Mall." *(All three, Canadian Pacific Archives, Montreal)*

Cathay Lounge.
This extraordinary room *(above and facing page)* by Edmund Dulac no doubt had its aesthetic origins in the later years of the nineteenth century, when Canadian Pacific was the leading passenger-carrying company between the Orient and Vancouver and the only scheduled means by which adventurous souls could complete round-the-world excursions. *(Both, Canadian Pacific Archives, Montreal)*

Jacques Cartier Room.
The *Empress of Britain*'s dining room—
named for the early French explorer of
what would become Canadian waterways—
was otherwise a tribute to Charles Rennie
Mackintosh and his Glaswegian school of
designers who gave modern furniture an
ancient grace and brought to the woodwork
of modern rooms the brute classicism of
English interiors as far back as the mead-
halls of Beowulf. *(Illustration from Canadian Pacific Archives, Montreal)*

Despite her many felicities of decor and the sense she communicated of power proudly borne, the *Empress of Britain* remains a forgotten wonder, a beloved figure in a dream of the past to those whose affections match their discriminations. Who is to say why? Was she an unwelcome ghost of the Great Depression? A victim of the chauvinist thoughtlessness that regards anything Canadian as derivative or marginal? An offensive barge of pleasure, floating the rich beyond the range of hardship and despair? Or was she simply too beautiful to be believed? Her Jacques Cartier Room was a restaurant of light-oak elegance, lighthearted panelings and frescoes, carpeted with cushiony *moquette* light to the step. In her Mayfair Lounge a vaulted ceiling, supported by columns of jade-green marble, recalled the highest aspirations of the days of Charles Mewès and Arthur Davis. Her Empress Ballroom was spacious enough to allow for imperial waltzes reflected in mirrors designed to give the illusion of Versailles.

Through all of her rooms ran lingering echoes of Art Nouveau before it had succumbed to the lightning-bolt abstractions of Art Deco. Not since the *George Washington* and the *Kronprinzessin Cecilie*, more than twenty years earlier, had a ship's interiors been marked so delicately by the simplicities of decoration and the ingenuities of woodwork produced under the auspices of Charles Rennie Mackintosh and his disciples in ateliers from Scotland to England and across the continent to Prague and Vienna.

This revival in maritime terms of an Anglo-Scottish mode of interior decoration might have been

Not Pompeii, Glasgow.
The cloistering vision of Mackintosh comes into its purest expression in the severely sober swimming pool of the *Empress* and the immovable turtle that brings a welcome sense of scale to its austerity. *(Both, Canadian Pacific Archives, Montreal)*

anticipated. Brangwyn had taken his early training with Mackintosh's master, William Morris, and had worked in Morris's studios. Lavery, beginning his painting career in Glasgow, went on to become the leading exponent of "the Glasgow School." Dulac, a Frenchman, had no professional Glaswegian connection; but he had brought to illustrations of English books a cosmopolitanism which, once more in evidence on the *Empress*, was useful counterpoise to the amiable parochialism that might have otherwise dominated Canada's first and last great liner.

A ship out of epoch, the *Empress of Britain* lived and died as if unaware that she extended the virtues of an older dispensation and might have been the model and criterion of a new one. Barely ten years old and game to the end, she was sailing a dangerous yet familiar course in October 1940, when a long-range German bomber spotted her off the northwest coast of Ireland and set her afire. Two days later, while she was being towed to haven by a British rescue ship, a Nazi submarine came close enough to fire two torpedoes into her side. Like a *cathédrale engloutie*, she sits now in the depths of the same cold waters she was meant to ride.

Never achieving the aura of celebrity surrounding ships of lesser grace and amenity, and without setting up record-breaking expectations or claims of Babylonian splendor, the *Empress of Britain* was perhaps the most confidently grand liner of the century. Indifferent to tabloid glamour and the evanescence of what might pass for transatlantic chic, she disappeared into history as quietly as she had arrived. In the large account of life on the oceans, she looms and recedes like a figure out of myth—the White Sister of the North, a legend still in the making.

Sailing Down the River.
Before the discovery in the late forties of the pertinent properties of the anti-histamine C_{17}, $H_{22}NO.C_7H_6ClN_4O_2$, called dymcnhydrinate, that would prevent or control seasickness, Canadian Pacific made much of the fact that nearly a third of an *Empress* crossing would be made in the calm waters of the St. Lawrence River and the Gulf of St. Lawrence. *(Right, Mark Goldberg Collection)*

IL DUCE AND "ITALIA" —
THE SHAPES OF THINGS TO COME

Fasces and Baldacchino.
Under imperial trappings, Il Duce's invited guests—including King Victor Emmanuel III, his Queen Elena, and the Archbishop of Genoa—assemble to witness the launching of the *Rex* from an unorthodox position on her starboard flank instead of at her prow. The transatlantic liner as an emblem of national pride—from the time of Kaiser Wilhelm II to the ill-chosen day, September 3, 1939, when Eleanor Roosevelt christened U.S. Line's *America*—was never more ardently promoted than in the middle years of Italy's Fascist regime. *(Illustration from Mark Goldberg Collection)*

Throughout the twenties, Italy on the high seas, comfortable in its tassels-and-tesserae parochialism, was largely an Italian affair. This held true also for operations in what the early Romans and Mussolini called *mare nostrum*—"our sea." There, ships as overstuffed and overwrought, if not as large, as Atlantic liners crisscrossed to and from Naples, Genoa, and the Mediterranean ports of North Africa with a flair never more deftly documented, or more lovingly re-created, than in Federico Fellini's operatic spoof, *E la Nave Va (And the Ship Sails On)*.

By the early thirties, however, when the antiquarian charms of the *Saturnia* and *Vulcania*, and the *bella figura* suavity of their tradition-conscious service personnel, had become known to travelers from America and Mittel-Europa, Italy was at long last in the transatlantic swim. Wartime setbacks aside, she would reach the point, forty years later, at which the fleet of white-hulled Italian liners in the Mediterranean and on the Atlantic routes to South and North America would embody and symbolize the last remaining wonder of the steamship era.

This ascension to an unprecedented place in the maritime picture was a development sparked by three widely diverse factors. First was the showmanship of Benito Mussolini with which he enlisted members of the royal House of Savoy to sponsor, launch, or otherwise endorse ships designed to stand for fascism afloat. Next was the quietly emergent mastery of Gustavo Pulitzer Finali in applying the lessons of the *Ile de France* and the *Bremen* to *arredo navale*. Finally, and most important, the recognition, especially by American travelers, that the "sunny southern route" was indeed a more pleasant and salubrious way to cross the Atlantic than by submission to days under steamer robes on windswept decks or to foggy incarceration at bridge tables.

Under Il Duce's shotgun persuasion, the three Italian companies operating in the North Atlantic, hit hard by the Great Depression, were united as of January 2, 1932, under one rubric—"Italia" Società Anonima di Navigazione—popularly known in Europe as "Italia" and in America as the Italian Line. When, in that same year, Pulitzer Finali's vision of a translation of old elegance into modern terms was triumphantly realized in the first crossing of the *Conte di Savoia* to New York, a course was set. Soon, by the transformation of once empty outdoor spaces into Lido Decks equipped with all the cabana amenities that went with the pool areas of resort hotels, other Italian ships anticipated that time, not far in the future, when the cruise would replace the crossing and "liners to the sun" would become destinations in themselves.

Lured by advertisements suggesting that life aboard was a matter of balmy nights and dazzling days—rare enough in any Atlantic season—Americans soon became aware that the even more distinctive feature of life on

Italian liners was the cheerful demeanor of well-trained crews and the pervasive sense of domestic intimacy this assured. Zest for a good table and the white-linen amenities of the nineteenth century gave the ships a combined air of opulence and hominess; and a characteristic open and unjudging curiosity about everything human on the part of their staffs was a welcome check to the kind of insouciant savoir faire characterizing the figures that populated the Italian Line's advertisements. Unlike workers on liners conceived in northern weather and Lutheran sobriety, the Neopolitans and Genovese who accepted the discipline necessary to the round-the-clock demands of great liners were not repressed by them. The ageless stewardesses of Cunard ships, for instance, with their flat shoes and flat faces, looked as though they might very well have been in the Crimea with Florence Nightingale. On an Italian ship, a passenger pressing his call button would likely be greeted in a few moments by a steward or stewardess, smartly tailored and self-assured, who'd receive his request, whatever it might be, with willingness, but also with a touch of unconcealed amusement.

This combination of brio and efficiency enchanted Americans. Soon, in the hundreds of thousands, they would be familiar with the sailing-day entreaties of stewards anxious to dispatch ashore the tipsy, the lovesick, or

Rich Kids.
Occupying a verandah suite and attended by a nursemaid in improbable skirts and apron, these privileged youngsters also had access to a playroom where they might be entertained by storytellers, puppet shows, even a miniature merry-go-ground. Such idealized renderings of familial domesticity—even in travel literature—were encouraged by Mussolini's Fascist state to promote his policies of population growth. Indeed, in 1932 E.N.I.T., Italy's official tourism promotion agency, offered incentives in the form of discount coupons for transportation and lodging to honeymooning couples.

(Right) Rex's two-deck-high chapel allowed for those traveling in other than First Class to attend, from the vantage point of the choir loft, daily mass. (Both, Mark Goldberg Collection)

the merely reluctant remnants of bon-voyage parties. As, trembling with power, the four-square *Vulcania* or the dashing *Rex* was all set to back out into the North River, the message was as urgent as it was shrill. "*La nave è in partenza!*" the stewards would cry. "The sheep is *living!*"

Under their noses, the brothers Coppedè had for years harbored a renegade who would become a rival. His name was Gustavo Pulitzer Finali, and his transformations of domestic marine design and decoration would soon turn the Coppedèian *baroccheggiante* into comedy and make the ships fitted out by La Casa Artistica seem like aberrations waiting to be detected.

Triestino by birth, Pulitzer Finali was the son of a businessman whose forebears had long been part of Trieste's distinguished Jewish mercantile community. Educated in a school attended by the sons of the local *borghesia*, he then went on to Munich. There, as a student in the Polytechnikum, he was awarded a diploma in engineering, in lieu of a diploma in architecture—a subject not yet certified by that institution.

In terms of his future, Pulitzer's most important scholastic advantage at the Polytechnikum was the chance

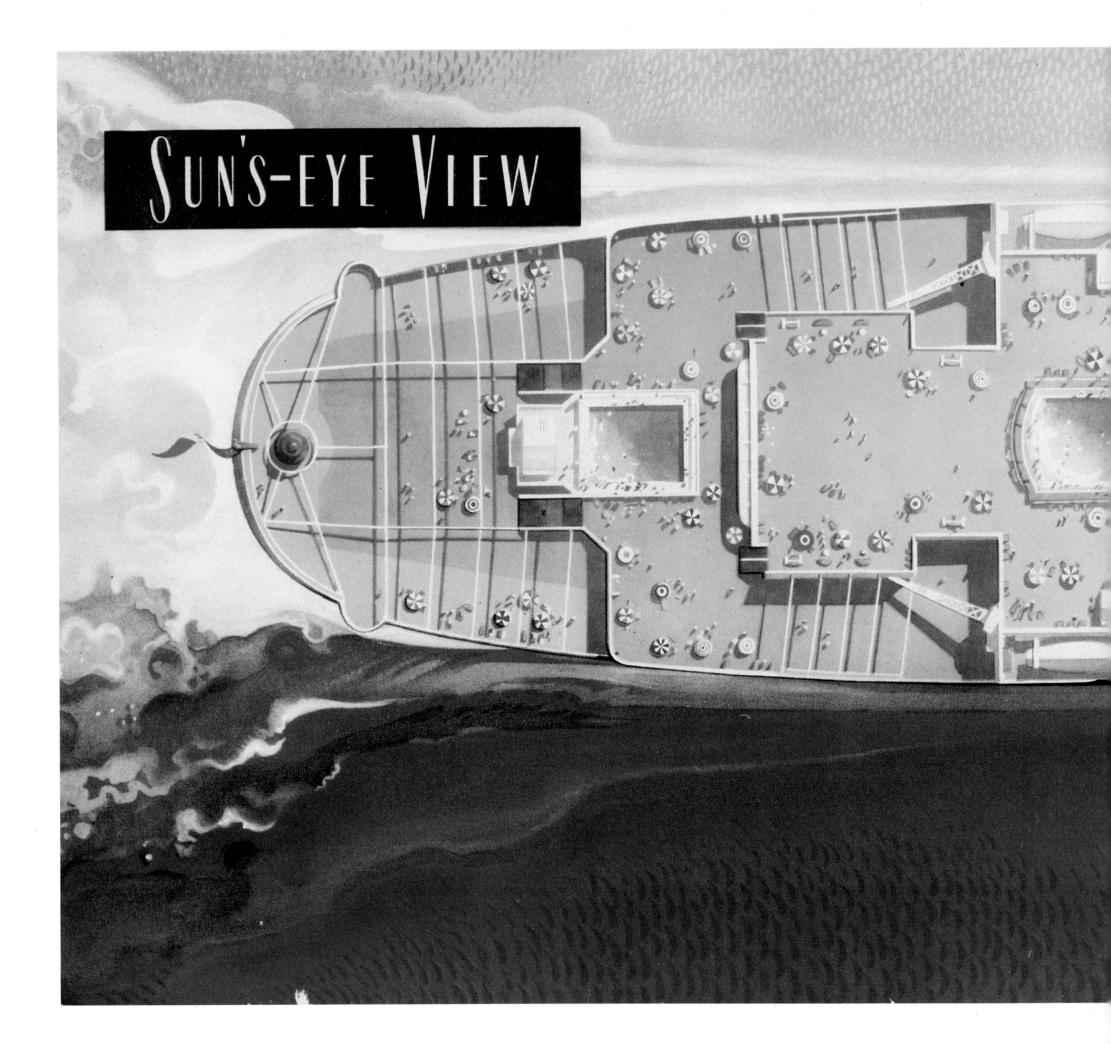

SUN'S-EYE VIEW

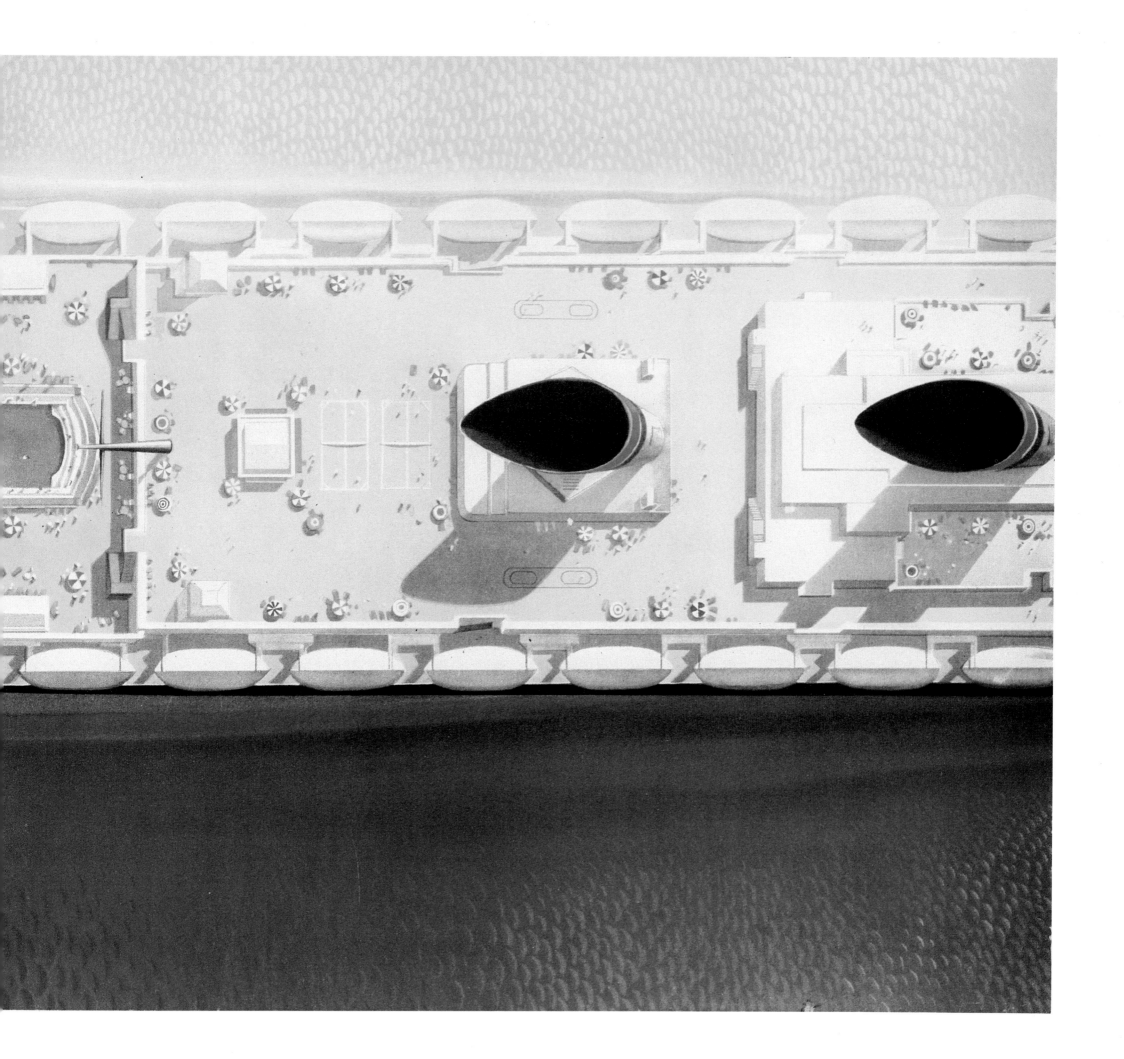

Aquatic Marvel.
Lavish though it was—encircled with bronze, flanked by princely cabanas, and with real beach sand dumped at its edges—*Rex*'s pool, seen here after sundown, did not—regardless of the illustrator's exaggeration—hold enough water to meet the daily needs of the smallest of Italian towns.

Atlantic Playground.
(*Preceding pages*) The sun's-eye view of the *Rex*'s Lido Deck, slightly larger than life but true to the spirit of a Southern Route crossing on Mussolini's consolidated "Italia" Line in the 1930s. The single development attending the penultimate phase of ocean travel was the blossoming of Italian liners as floating resorts aboard which life took place largely out of doors on sea-lanes that skirted the Azores and rounded the Rock of Gibraltar. Cruise-crossings, really, they made it possible to step aboard a ship in New York—or Boston—and, sixteen relaxing days later, step off in Venice or Trieste.

to study with architect Theodor Fischer, a fifty-year-old veteran of the ideological skirmishes in the world of arts and crafts that marked the last years of the nineteenth century and continued into the twentieth. Once conservative, Fischer had remained faithful to the historical eclecticism of his time until, *volte-face*, conversion to the Secessionism, *razionalismo*, and other manifestations of the new spirit in art led him to become a founder, in 1907, of the influential Deutscher Werkbund and one of the most articulate proselytizers in the cause of Jugendstil. Under his aegis, Pulitzer was introduced to the theories reflecting aesthetic impulses which, lighting up the landscape of Europe like brushfires, had burned away all but the last relics of the cultural insularity on which the Coppedès had based their collective career.

Travel on the Continent and in England further acquainted Pulitzer with contemporary innovations; and then, sketching his way through Tuscany, Umbria, and Emilia, he returned to Trieste with copiously illustrated notebooks, and perhaps a grudging tolerance for the care and bravado with which the Coppedès had made their antiquarian borrowings.

When he accepted a commission to work with the brothers on the *Conte Grande*, Pulitzer was for reasons of his own unwilling to rock the Coppedè boat. He seemed, in fact, to have joined in the Coppedèian spirit of things with an enthusiasm suspiciously close to vengeance. Charged with the design of the *Conte*'s indoor swimming pool, he produced a *fantasia orientale* which, however far-fetched as a public space on an Italian ship, at least erased for all time the cliché that swimming pools were, by nature, exclusively Pompeiian.

One end of this pool featured two green lions "of a Buddhist disposition" which, between an opening in a lacquered bridge, spouted fans of water into the pool itself. At the other end, a hanging garden dropped its blossoming vines into a space between a Japanese paper wall and balusters supporting a marble bench placed atop a slab of marble forming a sort of decorative dam. The area was lighted overall through tent-like panels of canvas and defined, on the lengthwise sides of the pool, by cribhouse-like changing rooms, each with a brightly painted door.

Working in the camp of the enemy, as it were, Pulitzer nevertheless distinguished himself—particularly in the eyes of a naval architect who had become a maritime tycoon, Nicolo Costanzi. Director of Trieste's great shipyard, the Cantiere Navale di Monfalcone, Costanzi had both the vision and the means to take Italian shipbuilding in one leapfrog advance from the era of the liner as a period piece to that of the liner as a paradigm of technology. Under his sponsorship, Pulitzer Finali was able to escape the constrictions of the Coppedè preserve and, on his own, proceed to oversee the decoration of two ships—the *Victoria* and the *Conte di Savoia*—each indelibly associated with his name and with the entirely unanticipated ascension of Italy to supremacy on the Atlantic.

Unfortunately, the *Victoria* has no place in the chronicles of transatlantica. The fastest motorship ever built, she was never tested in the Blue Riband stakes, or subjected to the kinds of impressionistic report and stylistic enumeration that allowed other ships to take on the air of personalities. In passenger ship development, however, the *Victoria* represents a crucial link among the *Bremen* of 1929, the *Conte di Savoia* of 1932, and, by extension, the Italian and American ships that would carry the refinements of modernism across the ancient sea-roads of the Mediterranean and into the twilight of the ocean-liner era. Remembered as "the white arrow of the Mediterranean," the *Victoria* arrived as an anachronism and departed as a paragon. As far as passenger ships were concerned, Italy in 1930 had barely left the nineteenth century. All of a sudden, Italians could claim the most advanced example of what the ship of the twentieth century might come to be.

Big, fast, burdened with symbolism and doomed to disaster, the most famous liners Italy would ever launch made their first voyages to New York between June and November of 1932. Slightly larger and decisively more swift, the *Rex* from Genoa came first, followed by the sister ship from Trieste in whose shadow she was destined to live—throughout her own career and in the judgment of history. The point of difference was aesthetic. The *Conte di Savoia*'s interiors were the product of a designer at the apex of his maritime career, Gustavo Pulitzer Finali.

Final Flourish.
Painters apply gilding to the three-foot-high letters of the name chosen for Lloyd Sabaudo's last *Conte* liner. Launched by the Genoese firm in October of 1931, the new flagship became a part of Il Duce's "Italia" Flotta Riunite before the scheduled maiden voyage. Utterly modern in silhouette, *Conte di Savoia* had a cruiser stern, the world's first seagoing gyro-stabilizer, and an enclosed promenade *(facing page)* almost 400 feet long—not as long as the *Bremen*'s, but far exceeding her rival in total glass area. *(Promenade, Mark Goldberg Collection)*

Those of the *Rex* were entrusted largely to the Studio Ducrot of Palermo, at whose threshold the twentieth century had received a bow, but no invitation to enter.

Each with two huge raked funnels far forward, the *Rex* and the *Conte di Savoia* had black hulls cradling the most advanced of contemporary power plants and tiered white superstructures laid out, stem to stern, like summer resorts. Prodigies of shipbuilding excellence in a decade of maritime accomplishment never to be paralleled, they were also, willy-nilly, advertisements for Italian fascism in the years before most Americans realized that Mussolini's vaunted timetable efficiency obscured political aims that would appall them. Il Duce's minister of communications left no doubt about the propaganda importance of the new wonder ships. "The great liners which, after the first decade of the Fascist Regime," said Costanzo Ciano, "have now entered into the great field of competition represented by transatlantic traffic are genuine exponents of the discipline, technique, and spirit of enterprise of the New Italy. They represent the combined result of all the efforts which we have made during the last ten years to recapture Italy's legitimate position on the seas."

Whatever this "legitimate position" was supposed to be, the bombast in which it is cited attempts to carry a day that might, more legitimately, be devoted to recollections of Christopher Columbus, Andrea Doria, Amerigo Vespucci, and Giovanni da Verrazano.

Perhaps Mussolini had such considerations in mind when he went to Genoa to inspect the *Rex* and, within hours of the start of her maiden voyage, take lunch aboard. In the event, his blessing proved to be no help at all. The *Rex*'s first voyage was stopped all but cold before she got even as far as Gibraltar. There, with two of her three turbogenerators inoperative, she had to wait almost four days before repairs allowing her to continue could be made. Scores of her passengers had meanwhile sought other arrangements. Mayor Jimmy Walker of New York and his entourage headed by train to France in order to catch the *Europa* at Cherbourg. Others accepted the

Gustavo Pulitzer Finali.
The man from Trieste *(above)* and his proposal *(right and facing page)* for refurbishing Navigazione Generale Italiana's *Roma* of 1926. The radical remodeling, in this instance, was not carried out, but Pulitzer Finali succeeded elsewhere in introducing his version of the International Style into the hitherto impenetrable precincts of the brothers Coppedè and the deep-seated parochialism of Italian shipbuilders. *(Pulitzer Finali and drawing, courtesy of Donato Riccesi, Trieste; right from "Italia" Navigazione, Genoa)*

opportunity to make a slower but steadier passage to New York aboard the *Vulcania*. Most of them, however, were willing to put up with dim lighting, lack of elevator service, and plumbing mishaps in order to be on hand when, however late and sheepish, the *Rex* passed the Statue of Liberty.

For all the tribulations and embarrassment of her debut, within the year the *Rex* had become the first liner from a Mediterranean port ever to capture the Blue Riband. On a voyage in August 1933, and on a course measured from Tarifa on the southwest coast of Spain to Ambrose Lightship, she crossed the Atlantic in 4 days, 13 hours, 58 minutes, and so wrested from the *Bremen* the mythical banner she had been entitled to fly for more than four years. While the *Rex* could never duplicate her record-breaking performance on an eastward passage, or for long hang on to the Nastro Azzurro, she had made it clear that Italian engineering and seamanship, if not Sicilian decor, were new factors in the Atlantic picture.

But the most abiding contribution of Italy to sea travel was the idea of a ship conceived as a floating resort. Alike in their broad sweeps of open deck and outdoor swimming pools surrounded with all the appurtenances the word *Lido* calls to mind, the *Rex* and *Conte di Savoia* were buoyed by a new wave of sun-loving voyagers in no hurry to get anywhere. These, for the most part, were Americans whose patronage gradually changed Atlantic crossings from socially uptight weeks indoors to laid-back runs of days when, half-dressed and one way or another half-soaked, they could share the *dolce vita* anonymity of guests at a resort hotel.

Side by side, the new ships gave no indication that, inside, one of them would reveal the most complete translation of modernism into elegance yet conceived, while the other would show herself to be a vast reliquary of the arts and crafts of the eighteenth century "interpreted" for contemporary consumption. Except for a wicker-and-treillage winter garden assigned to Roberto Giannini, an aging designer from Pistoia, the decorative spirit of the *Rex* was that of pre-Napoleonic Italy when, *palazzo* by *palazzo*, villa by villa, the scattered duchies and Papal States of the peninsula competed for status with the same zeal which, centuries later, made the golf-club suburbs of New York and Los Angeles settings for Norman châteaus, Swiss chalets, and Mexican haciendas.

Decoratively speaking, the *Rex*, like the *Bremen*, was the victim of a divided perception of what the eponymous liner of the century might be. Oblivious to the aesthetic grace that sets one ship apart from another, those who conceived the *Rex* produced a machine that belonged to the future and a floating hotel that belonged to the past. Unfortunately, theirs was not authentic history, but a version of it alternately reduced and inflated. Once more, those unable to comprehend the integrity of the past were among the first to plunder its effects.

For Pulitzer Finali, the step from the *Victoria* to the *Conte di Savoia* was a giant one, and he took it without breaking stride. An amplified version of the earlier ship, the *Conte di Savoia*, nearly twice as long and of a tonnage almost four times as great, repeated the linear simplicity of the *Victoria* and extended the cool sobriety of her classic Art Deco into a masterpiece. Except for one well-noted and all but grotesque intrusion—the Galleria Colonna with its enormous ceiling painting copied from Lucchesini's *Battle of Lepanto*, and its adjoining starboard chapel and portside soda fountain—the *Conte di Savoia* was the ultimate example of an aesthetic philosophy in which coherence and *razionalismo* were prized above shows of opulence or indulgences in whimsy.

No small part of that philosophy was an openness to the international spirit of the times and the freemasonry of exchange it encouraged. The striking similarity of Pulitzer Finali's Smoking Room on the *Conte di Savoia* to Rudolf Schröder's on the *Bremen* was no doubt observed with pleasure by travelers who, unlike critics of design, are more interested in results than in origins. Other near duplications—like the tall oval windows of the *Bremen* that were echoed on the sun deck of the *Victoria*—perhaps confirm the truth of the notion that, in the arts, genius steals what talent merely borrows.

In any case, one of the most felicitous things about Pulitzer Finali's "adaptations" was the use he made of indirect lighting to unite and, at the same time, to dramatize their reductive simplicity. His ceilings—curved, rounded, domed, rectangular, but always low—emanated the warmth essential to rooms less dependent upon decoration than upon proportion to give them charm. Consequently, the *Conte di Savoia's* interiors—line,

Before the Fact.
This preliminary sketch by Pulitzer Finali for the *Conte di Savoia*'s dining room shows a warmer color scheme than finally obtained and a lively fountain which, in the event, was displaced by an indirectly lit circular buffet *(above)* of greater practicality but considerably less charm.
(Designer's original watercolor courtesy of Donato Riccesi, Trieste)

volume, and spatial relationships—emphasized Pulitzer's architectural gifts in a way that made the idea of decoration in a traditional sense redundant.

As if to deny his point, or to expose its politically suspect "cosmopolitanism" (a fascist euphemism for Jewish influence), Gino Coppedè's Galleria Colonna somehow found a place on this most advanced of ships and thus added a touch of decorative schizophrenia to her otherwise unquestionable attributes. The *Conte di Savoia*'s grand saloon, in spite of its archaeological fidelity to the decor of the Roman *palazzo* from which it was derived, remains an anachronism explicable only on the basis of "special interest."

Never among those to permit their financially powerful connections off the hook when the advancement or retention of their primacy was at risk, the Coppedès, with a little help from old sponsors, muscled their way into a ship that was, aesthetically speaking, none of their business and thus supplied her with a feature widely deplored and pictorially irresistible. Ironically and, in the circumstance, incongruously, the Galleria Colonna became more famous than any other room aboard the first unequivocally modern liner.

Baffling to the layman and all but inexplicable to the maritime observer, its place aboard the *Conte di*

Bow Windows.
Unique on the sea-lanes, Pulitzer Finali's upper-deck suites featured protruding bays providing not only floods of daylight through unapologetically ship-shaped windows but sea views fore and aft. *(Courtesy of Donato Riccesi, Trieste)*

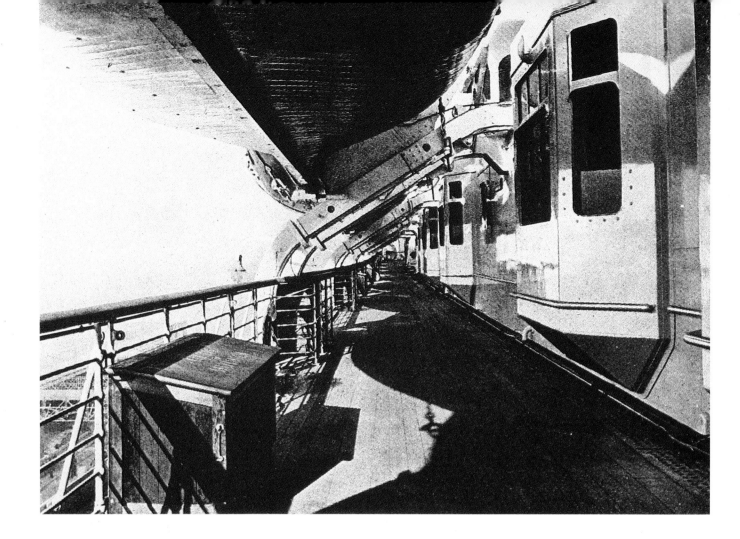

Galleria Colonna.
Reproduced with an almost archaeological fidelity (save for the obtrusively contemporary zebra-striped sofas and chairs), the *Conte di Savoia*'s grand saloon came piecemeal from an ancient Roman *palazzo*.

Its presence on a ship generally regarded as the most technologically advanced and decoratively avant-garde liner of her time is explicable only as a response by some of her builders to the insistence of some of her intractably conservative owners. *("Italia" Navigazione, Genoa)*

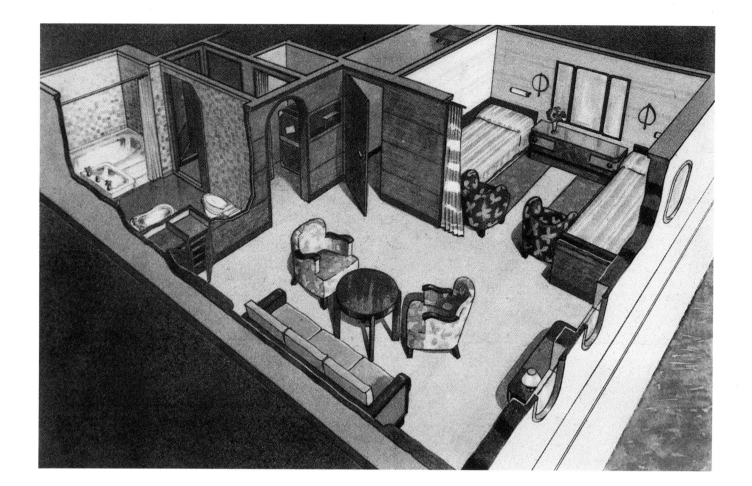

Living Room.
As Atlantic liners began to shrink the differences between classes in the way of comfort, plumbing facilities, and menus, they began to expand the kinds of accommodations available in First Class to the point that the only thing separating big spenders from their less affluent shipmates was the amount of cubic space they occupied. A minor advantage at first, space—as exemplified by this *apparta-mento di lusso* on the *Conte di Savoia*—would become the one and only "extra" the sea traveler could buy, in both living and dining quarters.

Savoia might best be accounted for by Donato Riccesi, a fellow townsman and biographer of Pulitzer Finali. "The reproduction, even on a reduced scale," he says, "of the baroque *salone*, all brocade, plaster, gilt, frescoes, statues, and columns of precious marble, omits all nautical references, and at the same time cloaks the structure of the ship in a monumental and false mantle.

"The execution of this stylistic anachronism, both inside and out, much more apparent in a ship with lines so significantly modern, was a response to heavy pressure on the part of the client, who insisted upon a historical flourish, at least in the atmosphere of the ship—so very important—in deference to the traditional style of ship decor, which had not yet wholly vanished at the beginning of the thirties."

As an authentic reproduction of a *salone* in Rome's Colonna Palace, the Galleria in its maiden voyage freshness apparently commanded respect enough to withstand charges of "stylistic anachronism" and no doubt others calling attention to the disparity between the overall modernity of the *Conte* and the museum piece that became her centerpiece. But when the directors of "Italia" furnished the room with the zebra-striped upholstery familiar to patrons of Manhattan's famous El Morocco nightclub and its imitators, this ceased to be true. Widely pictured, the Galleria became the prime example of the antiquarian garishness that, to generations of Americans, seemed to issue from the studios of the Mamma Leone Academy of Design.

Imposed upon, short-lived, and ill-fated, the *Conte di Savoia* nevertheless established herself as the handsomest and most technologically advanced Italian liner of her time. Spare, elegant, and responsive to every nuance in the vocabulary of decoration, she did not so much recapture history as make it.

PART SEVEN

Climax and Conclusion:
The Grandest Way to Cross

Second Class.
Travelers on the *Normandie* so reduced in circumstance as to have to forgo her finer accommodations had no recourse but to take their meals in this dining room and hope to survive on menus austerely limited to six or seven courses.

Grand luxe—a tentative offering that soon produced an enduring demand—would continue to be available on the ocean for many years after "the transatlantic style" had become a parody of itself sometimes approaching travesty. Strictly speaking, *grand luxe* had nothing to do with style; it simply stood for the best that money could buy in the way of amenity, including that most coveted of shipboard commodities, private space. The transatlantic style, on the other hand, was a broad and many-faceted reflection of the servant-surrounded life maintained by the rich when "society" was a preserve of grace and privilege recognized even by those who paid little attention to the hometown society page, or to the doings of the ubiquitous "society lady." When society in the old sense disappeared into the political and economic reshufflings of World War II, with it went most of what made the notion of a transatlantic style tenable.

Before this happened, however, travel on the Atlantic, already marked by notable refinements of *grand luxe* in its German and Italian versions, entered a phase of fantasy and grandiosity entirely without precedent. In the 150-year chronicles of scheduled sailings between the New World and the Old, nothing previously imagined or built had or would surpass, or even remotely approach, the size, power, and Tiberian sumptuousness of the *Queens—Mary* and *Elizabeth*—or of the *Normandie.* Superships of an era that would come to its end when they did, they entered history in an aura of glory all too soon made ironic by history itself. The irony lay in the circumstance. At almost the very moment when ocean liners reached a zenith of technological sophistication and the uttermost expression of the ship conceived as a palace, a grand hotel, or a floating city, they became obsolete with a finality that would soon render them extinct. History had decreed that a great and ever expanding phase of human enterprise would reach a climactic conclusion at its finest hour and most exquisite point of success.

R. M. S. QUEEN MARY—
"THE STATELIEST SHIP…"

Reigning Queens.
Speaking of the woman, Cecil Beaton reminds one of the ship: "Queen Mary," he said, "created an appearance for herself that served as an all-weather model, good for rain and shine. Wherever one saw her, everything about her neat silhouette was as compact and tidy as a ranunculus. You knew that you were in the presence of royalty; and, with true noblesse oblige, she was always reliable in her appearance, never letting you down, but turning up regularly with mechanical precision upon any occasion, however small."

Like Beaton's description of the woman whose name she took, the R.M.S. *Queen Mary* was regal without asserting prerogatives except those that accrued to her innate distinction. Like her patron, she had a somewhat wayward approach to fashion excused, or forgiven, by generations of devoted travelers who feel that her dedication to the rank and office of queen of the seas has not been superseded to this day. *(Interior courtesy of Ted and Joan Hindmarsh)*

Like many famous women in history, the most beloved ships have seldom been the most beautiful. Among these is the *Queen Mary*—the last Cunarder to keep the tall-hatted profile and dynastic air of self-sufficiency that had for long distinguished the line's ships and proved how dowdiness in the service of character could sweep all before it.

What endeared the *Queen Mary* to Americans no less than Britons and the high-ranking Soviets who made her their floating preserve remains a mystery time is not likely to unravel. If class, in the sense of distinction, is an endowment, she was blessed with it from the first. If class is a kind of unignorable presence recognized before it is defined, she had that too. Travelers who embodied distinction were at once at ease with her curious mixture of insistent Englishness and dubious modernism and remained faithful to the seagoing milieu they themselves created.

What the *Queen Mary* emanated was the pride of a century-old tradition oblivious to incursions of the transitory. Her room stewards still knew what clothes brushes, hatboxes, and collar buttons were for; her dining stewards neither lifted an eyebrow at idiosyncratic readings of the menu nor addressed those whom they served by their given names. From the "tiger" who acted as liaison man in extending the courtesies of the captain's table and the captain's quarters to favored passengers, down to the "boots" who polished and returned before dawn the shoes put outside cabin doors at midnight, the *Queen Mary*'s service staff stayed inflexibly in the nineteenth century. Their intransigence was a matter of neither defiance nor whimsy. Dominating the ship's personnel were the working elite of Southampton, the "Cunard Yankees." These were the men and women who, ingrained for generations with their own sense of stewardship, quietly accorded American passengers a gentility not all of them possessed and a kind of noblesse-oblige authority few Americans would ever themselves assume. With British passengers, on the other hand, relations did not have to be established. When the Earl of Warwick was ready to put on his dressing gown, it was there.

Toward the encroachments of ever expanding "hotelism," the *Queen Mary* was somehow impervious. In blueprint, parts of her may seem to have been transported piecemeal from the Savoy, the Dorchester, and the Waldorf Hotel in the Aldrych. But she was, foremost, a ship at sea: brassbound portholes established the fact, and wooden deck chairs with blankets of navy blue lined with scarlet confirmed the vanishing pleasure of it. The gongs that called her passengers to dinner with "The Roast Beef of Old England" echoed the same notes heard by Charles Dickens on his way to Boston aboard the *Britannia* in 1842. Neither a boast nor a newfangled threat

Depression Relict.

Born in the depths of what the British called "the slump," the *Queen Mary* was but partly completed when, abandoned on the stocks of John Brown's shipyard, she sat for more than two years at the mercy of Clydeside weather and the thousands of rooks that made her battlement of a hull their nesting ground. Meanwhile, said a labor leader, the Clyde was "like a tomb—not a tomb newly made but a tomb with a vast and inescapable skeleton brooding over its silence."

To save the day, His Majesty's Government, at the urging of Prime Minister Neville Chamberlain, used the abandoned monster "as a lever for bringing about a merger between the Cunard and White Star Lines." When their unification was agreed upon, a huge government subsidy made it possible for the *Queen Mary* to be ready for launching within six months. When the new Cunard-White Star liner made her maiden voyage in May 1936, rooms on the Theban scale of her Main Lounge gave her a character, almost as monumental as the *Normandie*'s, that would stamp for all time the nature of the supership and presage its all too imminent disappearance.

SPORTS DECK

SUN DECK

PROMENADE DECK
65

MAIN DECK

"A" DECK

"B" DECK

"C" DECK

"D" DECK

"E" DECK

"F" DECK

"G" DECK

"H" DECK

QUEEN MARY

G H DAVIS

Fireside.
Mythical beasts and alabaster urns lighted from within surround the Main Lounge's monumental electric fire. An incongruous reminder of the shilling-in-the-slot grates of "bed-sitters" in the vasts of London's Earls Court, this one nevertheless cheered many a winter evening on the North Atlantic.

to the order of things, the *Queen Mary* was the culmination of nearly a hundred years of English seamanship and Scottish engineering. Tall in the water she could cut like a knife or ride like a duck, she became and remained for all of her life what King George V said she was: "The stateliest ship now in being."

While she would eventually be categorized as one of the most celebrated artifacts of what would soon be known as Depression Modern, the *Queen Mary* in her time continued to be endowed by her international clientele with a smartness, an in-group exclusivity unapproached in the later phases of transatlantica. Rivaled in her first years of service by some of the greatest liners ever launched from continental shipyards, outshone by their streamlined dash and sumptuousness, she sailed among them as though determined to mind her own business, and outlasted them all . . . in fact, in social eminence, and in sentimental memory. Affection for the *Queen Mary*, then and now, is marked by a kind of absolutism quite beyond quiddities of discrimination or sobriety of judgment. At the very time when the *Normandie*, inside and out, was recognized as the supreme product of oceangoing enterprise, when the *Ile de France* and the *Bremen* were consolidating their already well-endorsed claims to "the steamship style," when the Lido Decks of the *Rex* and *Conte di Savoia* were turning one-way passages into cruises, the *Mary* remained "the only way to cross" for those surviving remnants of society that had not yet succumbed to the whelming tide of café society.

The *Queen Mary*'s sense of class—as distinguished from a sense of style—was part and parcel of that phenomenon of social affectation which for more than a century had made England the Western world's cynosure in those matters of propriety and seemliness that gave social grace its meaning and "to the manner born" its resonance. Yet, decoratively speaking, the great ship was a product of a kind of taste as misguided in its xenophobic parochialism and calendar-art banality as it was short-lived. In the retrospect of fifty years, credulity is strained to accept as fact the assessment, widely seconded in the popular press, of an apparently knowledgeable critic of design as he concluded his tour of the new supership. "It is difficult to rein the overmastering enthusiasm inspired by the interior," he said, "and if the following notes appear to be immoderately superlative in tenor, the charge must be laid at the door of those who have designed and executed the schemes which confront the privileged visitor. Brilliant in conception . . . the passenger spaces reveal, down to their smallest detail, a fine appreciation of aesthetic fitness. The modern influence undoubtedly exists, but rampant modernity has been studiously and successfully avoided."

To this one is tempted to say Amen . . . but not before pointing with suspicion to the ignorance its concluding sentence advertises.

The truth was that the sensibilities of those executives charged to see that the *Queen Mary* would set out in the fine array to which she was entitled were so far behind and below the sensibilities of those who built and crafted her as to constitute another order of perception. The directors of Cunard had gone so far as to send secret emissaries to St.-Nazaire in an effort to learn what surprises the *Normandie* might be getting ready to spring; and they had put other spies on one of the French ship's first crossings to New York. But whatever these snoops may

Great Hall.
Queen Mary's Cabin (First) Class Lounge.
(Courtesy of Ted and Joan Hindmarsh)

have disclosed about the wonders of the *Normandie*, their reports came either too late or without sufficient urgency to disturb the complacent progress of decorators who had already taken their cues from the cinema palaces of Leicester Square and the furniture show-windows of Tottenham Court Road. As a result, "the stateliest ship" (an epithet unanimously endorsed by maritime authorities who had studied her lofty bearing and seawise behavior) had to undergo the depredations of a brand of British taste which in two decades had progressed only from an unfocused historical eclecticism to that misapprehension of the modern which produces the modernistic.

With everything at stake in their new liner's inevitable confrontation with the *Normandie*, the British public was cheered to learn from professionals that the *Queen Mary* was "as docile as a yacht," and took to heart a discrimination offered by an observer from Denmark: "The French have built a beautiful hotel and put a ship around it. The British have built a beautiful ship and put a hotel inside it."

But those of His Majesty's subjects who had an early chance to learn just what the inside of the *Queen Mary* looked like were less cheered than dismayed. Art critic Clive Bell made a tour of her superstructure and described what he saw as "teddy bear." He praised the *Mary*'s handsome lines and architecture, but, he said, "inside awaits disappointment. Good wooden surfaces have been broken up and disfigured with what businessmen call 'art.' " Ugh! said a lady columnist: "Shiny rayon damask . . . engraved Dianas with streaming

The Restaurant.
Massively aglitter and reverberant with conversation, this dining hall was able to accommodate, at one sitting, a greater number of passengers than that of any other transatlantic liner before or since. Its cubic space was ample enough to have contained not only Cunard's first pioneer *Britannia*, but Columbus's *Niña*, *Pinta*, and *Santa Maria* as well.

One of its humanizing features was the use of rubber-wheeled trolleys *(above)* bearing "steamship rounds" of roast beef under retractable domes of silver; twenty kinds of bread, rolls, and muffins for breakfast; sculptured desserts on pastry-shop tiers, rolled to the table by stewards poised to slice, spear, and scoop.

Above the entrance was a metallically *moderne* mural across which a little crystal model of the *Queen Mary* tracked the progress of a voyage between New York's Pier 90 and Southampton's Ocean Terminal. *(Mural and facing page courtesy of Ted and Joan Hindmarsh)*

hair and big-eyed unicorns racing across mirrors. Hideously patterned carpets. Strip-lit Winter Gardens and rubber plants. Strip-lit dressing tables with beech-grained plastic laminates." "The general effect," said *Architect and Business News*, "is one of mild but expensive vulgarity"—an impression echoed by another journalist for whom the *Mary* was "outstandingly vulgar, overwhelmingly voluminous, and impressively voluptuous. Outwardly she is a very handsome lass. . . . Inwardly she is a riot of ostentation carefully executed in the Leicester Square style. . . . The workmanship is magnificent, the materials used are splendid, the result is appalling."

Concerned with questionable aspects of decor, these impeachments did not apply to the architectural disposition of available space, nor could they have. Less favored than Charles Mewès, his long-deceased partner, Arthur Davis and his new colleague, Benjamin Morris, lacked the advantage of planning a ship with divided funnel uptakes and consequently had to devise ways by which the *Queen Mary* might achieve something of the kind of uninterrupted walk-through space attained in the stem-to-stern openness of the *Bremen* and *Normandie*.

What they managed to do within this constriction was exemplary. Old-fashioned as the *Queen Mary* was in relation to ships of an emergent high-tech efficiency, she carried herself, thanks to Davis and Morris, with a palatial air of space to squander as striking as the buoyant grace of movement which made her a ship-lover's paradigm.

With three enormous funnel casings to disguise and work around, Davis and Morris plotted a prodigal use of cubic space that would show in self-contained units rather than in an interconnecting series. What they produced was spectacular: a restaurant seating more diners at once than any other passenger ship before or

Last Call.
A Clydebank work gang puts finishing touches to *Queen Mary*'s Forward Observation Lounge just prior to her first voyage in May 1936. Above the half-round cocktail bar a mural depicts the week-long celebration, just a year earlier, of George V's Silver Jubilee. It would be a new king, however, Edward VIII, who would conduct a stem-to-stern final inspection of the ship two days prior to her maiden crossing.

Verandah Grill.
Overlooking the *Mary*'s broad wake, this upper-deck dining room offered—at a price—quieter tables in the limited company of shipmates prepared to forgo First Class in favor of *grande luxe*. Its murals, the contribution of Doris—one of two "Mayfair socialite sisters" named Zinkeisen—struck Evelyn Waugh as "kindergarten work in flat, drab colours," but other passengers found them amusingly appropriate to a room designed for dinner-dancing and midnight rendezvous.

since; a Main Lounge of Theban proportions; a Smoking Room with ceilings so high and dimensions so broad as to intimidate any cigar-lover less eminent and hard-eyed than J. P. Morgan or Winston Churchill.

To enter the main dining room of the *Mary* was to be engulfed in an acre of napery glimpsed beyond a Watts Tower of fruit, glazed and fresh, and great cornucopias of straw spilling out other delicacies like honey from a horn. A well of light, three decks high, the room was demarked at one end by tall bronze doors and at the other by a glittering chart of the North Atlantic across which a crystal model of the *Queen Mary* herself—mechanically, if rarely accurately—informed diners of the latitude and longitude of each moment of their traversal of the Great Circle. Underlying the splendor of illuminated space was an anomaly: flooring of something called Korkoid. As trendily synthetic as its name, this substance, buffed to a high gloss, was patterned in big brown and beige squares laid diagonally across the width and length of the room. The effect was not unlike that of a duchess in flowing chiffon and sparkling tiara who, close up, is seen to be wearing jogging shoes.

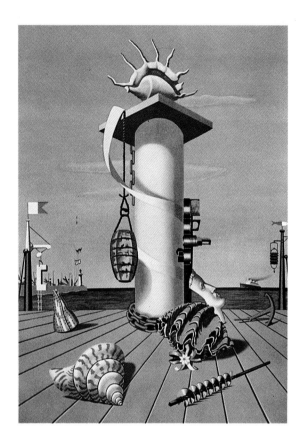

Daliesque Detritus.
It's "what business men call art," said the severest of British critics about this and others of the *Queen Mary*'s paintings and murals. Just as much of the ship's floorings and furniture had a look of the *moderne* translated into the idiom of Edgware Road, Edward Wadsworth's *The Sea* suggests a flagrant borrowing that transforms Salvador Dali's mysteriousness of displacement and distortion into a kind of pictorial cryptography hardly worth the trouble of deciphering.

Smoking Room.
(Facing page) Distinguished mainly by its extraordinary proportions, this still largely masculine preserve was weighted with chunky furniture upholstered in two-toned imitation leather and striped velour. Sparsely populated even on "heavy" sailings, its vast space in a well of light seemed to intimidate those whom it was most likely to invite. *(Both courtesy of Ted and Joan Hindmarsh)*

Perhaps the most stylistically cohesive room on the *Queen Mary* was the Observation Lounge—for many years an enclave reserved for First Class passengers and later transformed into a pub for Tourist Class with the cooperation of bartenders adept at making strings of paper cutouts and arranging displays of plastic genre art. This semicircle of silver-and-bronze-balustraded terraces, far forward, offered a panoramic, many-windowed view of weather ahead on one end and, on the other, A. R. Thomson's mural fantasy of democratic London—*The Royal Jubilee Week, 1935.*

The bar in this lounge, like most of those on ships, as well as on shore, was designed to provide the bartender with a full view of activities across the room, while limiting the view of patrons who sat on its red imitation-hide stools either to the figure of the bartender himself or to the hand-in-hand revels of viscountesses, shopgirls, debutantes, soldiers, and sailors in the mural overhead. What the bartender saw was a raised platform on which circular tables and chairs of laminated wood, trimmed with metal, were symmetrically placed on flooring of a substance called Ruboleum. Trough lighting on red-enameled pylons and the relentless circularity of everything in sight made the room a telling example of that moment in design history when the last lightning bolt and jagged edge of geometrical modernism began to submit to the more austere surfaces of high tech.

At a time when ships from the Continent featured First Class accommodations of enormous variety and even of individual uniqueness, cabins on the *Queen Mary* maintained a consistency of taste remarkable for its limited compass—from broom closet inside singles to Main Deck suites big enough to house, on more than one occasion, the personal entourages of Andrei Gromyko and Billy Graham. Each of these midships apartments was paneled in flitches of carefully split wood that looked like enormous Rorschach tests; but only the most expensive—"designed in the modern style, adequately restrained to secure a restful dignity"—contained the whole *marchés aux puces* conglomeration of period-piece objects that made the *Queen Mary* a tactfully undivulged embarrassment. These included electric grates on the order of the shilling-in-the-slot gas heaters familiar to tenants of an Earls Court "bed-sit"; voluminous bedspreads of glossily rugged chintz; electric clocks with hands that periodically jumped; plugs for curling irons; curtains of hugely flowered ivory satin appliquéd with pink and green ribbons; lamps of peach glass; tub chairs of two-toned leatherette. Of all of these accessories to aesthetic crime, swaths of python skin, used for decorative touches here and there, were probably the most imaginative and unexpected.

Except for the uncompromised metallic bleakness of the Observation Lounge in its first incarnation, modernism, rampant or otherwise, was indeed avoided in the *Queen Mary*. But what appeared in its place called for no congratulations, especially from a man to whom the twentieth century and all of its touted advances were an abomination. Speaking in the surrogate voice of Charles Ryder in *Brideshead Revisited*, Evelyn Waugh records his first impressions of the *Mary:* "I turned into some of the halls of the ship, which were huge without any splendor, as though they had been designed for a railway coach preposterously magnified. I passed through vast bronze gates whose ornamentation was like the trade mark of a cake of soap which had been used once or twice;

Decorative Wood.
Primitive figures in this wall panel suggest
the sources of the scores of exotic woods
inlaid throughout the public and private
rooms of the *Queen Mary*. Complementing
these, to the dismay of a lady columnist in
London, were "engraved Dianas with
streaming hair and big-eyed unicorns racing across mirrors."

Main Deck Cabin.
Laminated walls and boudoir bentwood
were standard features of the *Queen Mary*'s
best staterooms *(right and facing page)*, as
were indirect and neon lighting, along with
the bulbous little cups providing ventilation in the years before air-conditioning.
*(All three courtesy of Ted and Joan
Hindmarsh)*

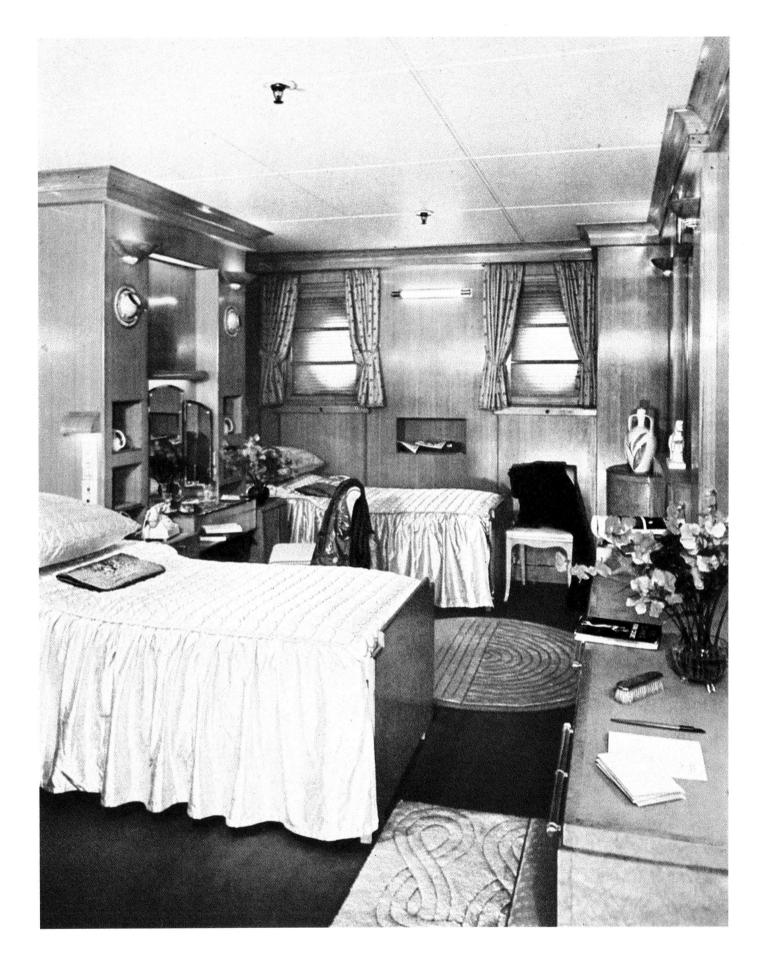

The Women.
Long after their successful penetration of
the once out-of-bounds Smoking Room,
women gained entrance to steam baths and
cooling rooms. Here, models promoting
the *Queen Mary*'s equal but separate
facilities foreshadow a time, decades in
the future, when an Atlantic voyage was
not only a place-to-place crossing but a
week's sojourn, should the passenger
desire, spent largely in a supervised health
spa.

Indoor Pool.
With breezy decks equipped for little more
than sea-gazing under steamer rugs, or
turns at shuffleboard, the *Queen Mary*
made much of her severely handsome
swimming pool and the chute that pleasantly ruffled its formality.

Boat Deck Aft.
The outdoor staircase on the right is one
of a symmetrical two leading into the
Verandah Grill. Aside from an illustrator's
exaggerated perspective, the clean sweep
of this deck was, at a glance, breath-
taking.

I trod carpets the colour of blotting paper; the painted panels of the walls were like blotting paper, too;
kindergarten work in flat, drab colours; and between the walls were yards and yards of biscuit-coloured wood
which no carpenter's tool had ever touched, wood that had been bent around corners, invisibly joined strip to
strip, steamed and squeezed and polished."

To some of those who today visit the gutted and inert remains of her in Long Beach, California, the *Queen
Mary* is a supreme period piece. To others she is a revenant whose visibility confirms her shape, size, and
bearing, yet obscures everything else about her that turned a once abandoned and rusting waif of the Great
Depression into a queen of the seas. In the durance vile in which, locked into inertia, she survives as a tourist
attraction and as a national monument sold for a price, she is still another reminder that the ash heap of history
is not without its scavengers. Who among her visitors, sated with statistics and burdened with the dreck available
in her shops, might sense the enchanted community she made when, skirted with foam of her own making, she
rode the sea-tracks of the Vikings from whom she was descended and arrived in New York or Southampton like a
miracle in which only she herself believed?

SHIP OF LIGHT—
LE GRAND PAQUEBOT NORMANDIE

Golden Touch.
(Facing page) A detail from one of the
lacquered panels in *Normandie*'s First
Class Smoking Room. The ship's wealth of
handcrafted opulence—from a Ruhlmann-
designed grand piano to chess tables
lacquered in crushed eggshell by Jean
Dunand—amply justified the claims of her
sponsors that she was a floating showcase
of the finest that France had to offer.
(Photograph by Olav Wahlund)

Provenance and Heritage.
Against a collage of all that produced her,
all that she would stand for—from the
façade of Nôtre Dame on the left to the
iron foot of Le Tour Eiffel on the right—
the *Normandie* treads for a moment the
waters she will triumphantly ride.

What Triumphal Way?
(Following pages) A watercolor by Albert
Brenet, master *célébrateur* of French Line
ships, captures the bright bustle of the
moment—6:40 P.M., Wednesday, May 29,
1935—when the *Normandie* began her
maiden voyage to New York. *(Courtesy of
Albert Brenet)*

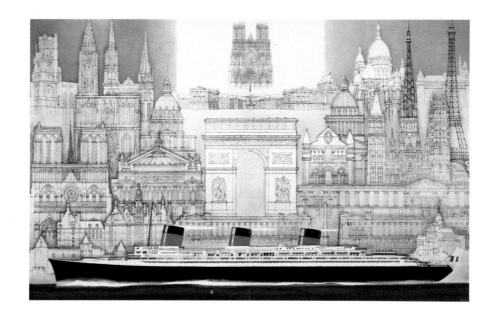

Style as Americans once knew it did not survive World War II. It became a collective memory: Fred Astaire in the kind of movement that looks like repose . . . the Chrysler Building's needle in the sky . . . Paul Robeson in the velvets of Othello . . . the huge, black-banded, and Sobranie-like funnels of an ocean liner without peer— the *Normandie*.

"Ship of light," they called her. The epithet, coined at a time when indirect lighting was novel, is less dithyrambic than descriptive. On the *Normandie*, light flowed from tiered pillars of Lalique, radiated from the depths of "fire pots" in the shape of funerary urns, glowed through fluted colonnettes and undulating panels, and otherwise coursed through the ship like a tree of nerves.

The means was glass—from the ductile walls of the Salle à Manger to the incised murals of the Grand Salon to the tubular arabesques of neon in the ceiling of the Café-Grill. The mirrors of Versailles were, after all, the most famous decorative objects in modern history. And where else but in France could one find the rose-window splendors of Chartres or the exquisitely attenuated arches of Ste.-Chapelle? The rationale for glass was lyrical. It is "so rich in clarity," said a designer, "so mercurial in its effects, so singing in its brilliance, so harmonic in its purity that it is almost alive."

A product of national pride, the *Normandie*, like her British rival, the *Queen Mary*, was inevitably burdened with the same symbolism. First, as a phoenix-like phenomenon rising out of the ashes of the Great Depression; next, as the highly visible emissary of a culture; finally, and unexpectedly, as the embodiment of a

Social Setting.

Early in the history of steamship development, passenger space was what remained after engine room, fuel bunkers, and cargo holds had been accommodated. By the time *Normandie* was launched, a revolution had occurred. The biggest ship in the world until 1940, French Line's masterpiece had an overall length of 1,030 feet, a beam of 118 feet, and funnel uptakes divided like tuning forks to allow an uninterrupted flow of space on her principal decks. Indeed, it was possible to stand on the stage of *Normandie*'s Promenade Deck theater (No. 42) and, all intervening doors being open, look through the length of the ship—through the Upper Elevator Hall, the Gallery-Lounge, the Grand Salon, the Smoking Room, the Café-Grill, and out across the terraced stern to the sea.

declining and doomed species. Both ships were floated on stupendous government loans, both caught the popular imagination in a way usually reserved for charismatic political figures or World Cup soccer teams. In the case of the *Normandie*, wonder and hope combined to make her launching an event *en grand apparat* celebrated with even more pomp and official attention than the ceremonious British could muster for the *Queen Mary*. Size, speed, and glamour were the most publicized of the new ship's attributes; but the passion that kept all of France on tenterhooks until the Blue Riband was unfurled into the breezes of New York Harbor was a sentiment expressed by an awed citizen in the form of a question: "What palace, what Triumphal Way, what memorial have we built to perpetuate our civilization, as the cathedrals perpetuate that of the Middle Ages, the castles of the Loire that of the Renaissance, and Versailles that of the age of Louis XIV?" The only answer was—the *Normandie*!

Propitious or unfortunate, the period in design history out of which the great ship came was marked by a

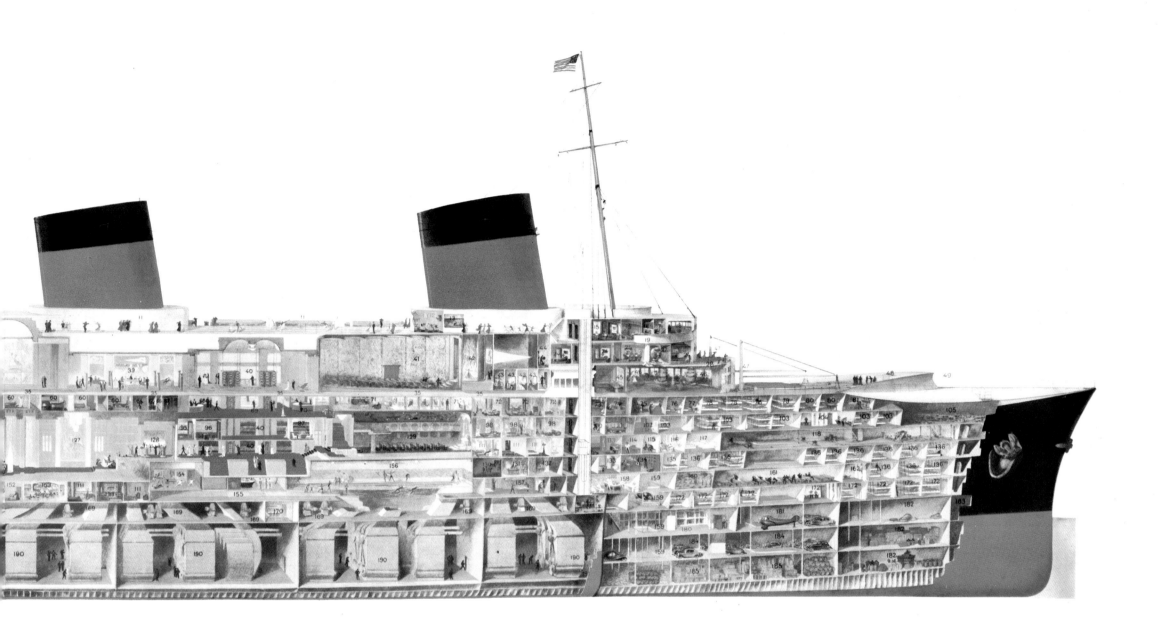

confluence of styles accepted, transitional, and imminently emergent. To some informed observers, the *Normandie* was the mature realization of marine Art Deco introduced by the *Ile de France* and unprecedented in the scope of its influence at sea and ashore. And a few of them noted with approval the breadth of taste that allowed for a strikingly modern chapel forward, a Bauhaus-derived nightclub aft, and a few metallic cabins of shipshape high-tech in between. Still others regarded the *Normandie* as an exhibition gallery dedicated to the programmatic and genre sentimentalism dear to a French middle class uncomfortable with—or indifferent to— the fact that Paris was the *fons et origo* of twentieth-century painting and sculpture.

In the nature of its wide-ranging *assemblage*, the decor of the *Normandie* supported and lent substance to each of these points of view. But in a perspective wide enough to incorporate all of them, the *Normandie* was a reassertion of the lavish and exalting "waste" of space characteristic of Beaux Arts architecture and answerable to its basic demand that life in public places be open, fluid, and touched with intimations of grandeur. Once she

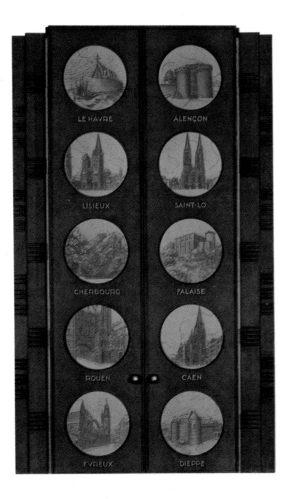

is regarded as belonging more congenially, if not irrevocably, to the company of Beaux Arts masterpieces—Paris's Opéra, for instance, or New York's Grand Central Terminal—than to the twentieth-century ships and structures that attempt to exploit space by confining it, her decorative schemes and the objects chosen to focus them fall into place. Homogeneous in spirit, however disparate in conception, the greatest of French liners was not, like the *Queen Mary*, a period piece of transitory affections embarrassed by time. Instead, she was a compendium of excellence in many modes posthumously recognized and only in recent years admired for the astonishing feat of unity in diversity that she was.

The genius of the *Normandie* was French in all respects but one—her exterior design. This was the triumph, muted to this day, of Vladimir Ivanovitch Yourkevitch, an émigré whose career with the Russian Imperial Navy was ended by the Revolution, whereupon he found his way to France. There, ten years later, working in a comparatively minor capacity at the Penhoët shipyards in St.-Nazaire, he drew up a design of hydrodynamic sophistication so compelling that company executives were moved to include, in the models they were testing for their new supership, one proposed by a man still regarded as an underling and outsider. When Yourkevitch's model outperformed all others in the Grenelle Tank of the French Admiralty and, later, in Europe's most exacting test tank in Hamburg, the commission for the exterior of the *Normandie* went to him, with results celebrated everywhere in the world—except in France. For reasons only speculation can supply, polite acknowledgment seemed then, as it does now, sufficient. Yet the imprint of Yourkevitch—recognized at once by his clipper bow and its gull-bone flanges, then by the broad esplanade of decking that runs unimpeded from the whale-back roofing forward to the step-down terraces aft—remains one of the most beautiful images of power in the service of grace to survive the steamship era.

From the moment the *Normandie* sailed out of Le Havre on May 29, 1935, what was left of High Society on the North Atlantic had found its new center—not of gravity, to be sure, but of a kind of elegance that decries frivolity even as the frivolous gains an ever larger role in the rituals of wealth and privilege from which it is officially excluded. Perhaps as brave as it was moribund, this last, war-shadowed attempt to "keep up the side" in a setting that still signified social eminence was kept lively by a factor which, always an aspect of ocean travel, now renewed itself with a flair. This was the theatricalism of voyages in which every passenger had a sense of playing a part in a production which, mounted in Le Havre or Manhattan for a short run, involved many costume changes, jostlings for the spotlight, and improvisations of speech and deportment inspired by a company gathered together for once, and once only. While a large complement of figures from show business—Maurice Chevalier, Marlene Dietrich, Cary Grant, Mistinguett, and Josephine Baker—supplied stars for these five-day productions, the obvious glamour of a *Normandie* crossing was of less importance to most passengers than the personal sense of having participated in a form of living theater. *Esquire* magazine's publisher and editor Arnold Gingrich attempted to describe this circumstantial euphoria. "You felt, once aboard the *Normandie*," he wrote, "not at home on it. . . . Home was never like this, and not that it belonged to you, but rather that you

Grand Entrance.
Normandie's Main Embarkation Hall left no doubt in the minds of arriving First Class passengers that they were boarding a ship of consequence. Rising in height two and a half decks, with walls clad in cream-colored Algerian onyx and accented with hammered glass and oxidized copper, the hall was served by four elevators running from swimming pool to theater. Gilded bronze doors at the aft end opened to the Main Dining Saloon. At the forward end, a huge cloisonné panel depicting a Norman knight marked the entrance to the ship's ecumenical chapel.

belonged to it. You felt . . . like a member of its cast, with a part to play. . . . The five-day passage was like one long big grand masked ball . . . with everybody either a Lady, or a Gentleman, and it never seeming to matter much who or what else."

Designers for the extraordinary stage setting which the *Normandie* came to be ranged from ultramodernists to antiquarians. What they had in common was the will and opportunity to work on a big scale within limits imposed only by their talents and a governing catholicity of taste that would make the *Normandie* the avatar of her own aesthetic moment. In charge of most of the ship's public rooms were four architects, working as two-man teams. Jean Patou—whose Pavillon d'un Collectionneur had been one of the outstanding structures of the great Art Deco exhibition of 1925—collaborated with Henri Pacon on the main entrance hall and dining room and laid out general schemes for the chapel, swimming pool, and stairways which other artists and artisans could work out in detail. A more important run of space was allotted to Roger-Henri Expert and Richard Bouwens—a team less hand-in-glove than Patou and Pacon, simply because Expert, whom someone dubbed "antique modernist,"

Son et Lumière.
Walls of light that warmed the busy dining
hour in *Normandie*'s Salle à Manger provided a theatrical centerpiece for the
concealed, indirect, diffused, suffused, or
otherwise ingenious networks of illumina-
tion that ran throughout the ship. Totally
windowless, the largest seagoing space to
be air-conditioned up to 1935, no other
room afloat has ever remotely approached
the sumptuous dazzle of the length,
breadth, and height of this one.

Cathedral Dimensions.
Punctuating the vista that overwhelms it, the commandant's table brings attention to the shape of *Normandie*'s restaurant *(above)* which, against a trend then current, placed all of its diners in one sweep of space rather than providing some of them with intimate alcoves or "dining areas." The eight private dining rooms—and the Banquet Room (not shown in plan)—were separate entities closed off by massive bronze doors from the central space.

The extraordinary amount of cubic space allotted to the principal public rooms of the *Normandie* is dramatized in the cutaway *(far right, facing page)* in which the transverse schematic view of the ship outlines the shape of divided uptakes from engine room to funnel.

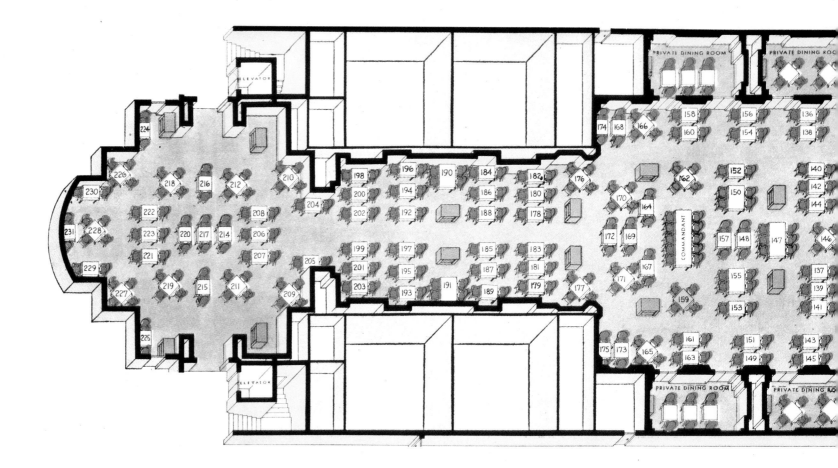

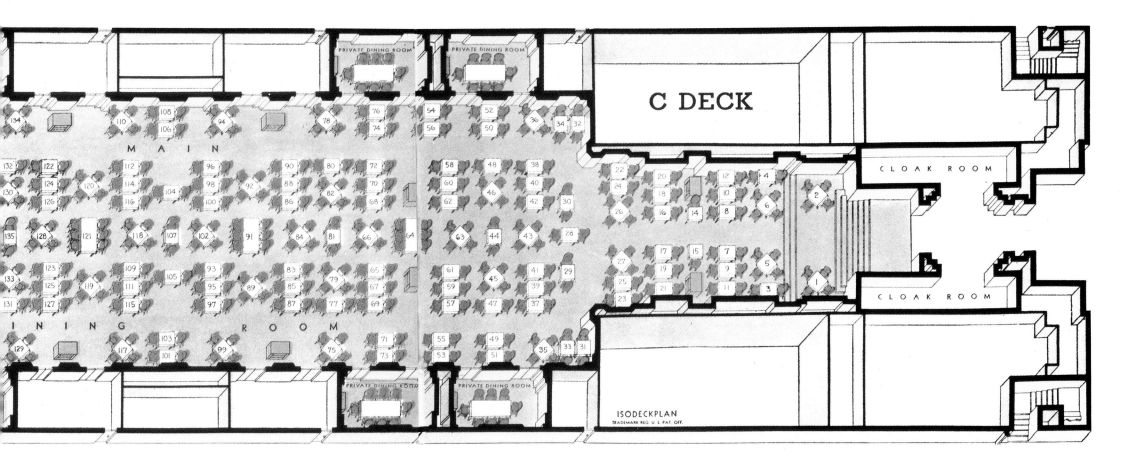

C DECK

CLOAK ROOM

CLOAK ROOM

PRIVATE DINING ROOM

PRIVATE DINING ROOM

MAIN

DINING ROOM

ISODECKPLAN
TRADEMARK REG. U.S. PAT. OFF.

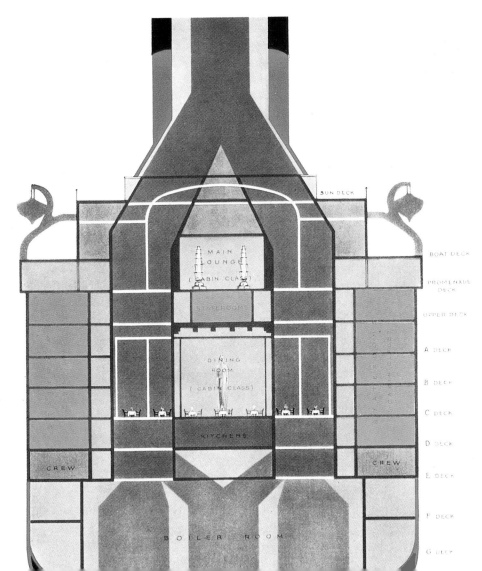

SUN DECK

BOAT DECK

MAIN
LOUNGE
(CABIN CLASS)

PROMENADE
DECK

STATEROOMS

UPPER DECK

A DECK

DINING
ROOM
(CABIN CLASS)

B DECK

C DECK

KITCHENS

D DECK

CREW

CREW

E DECK

F DECK

BOILER ROOM

G DECK

was of a more flexible disposition than his aging partner whose work, wholly answerable to establishment expectations, had consisted largely of commissions from bankers to produce impressive, sometimes awesome, banks. In effect, the *Normandie* was put into the hands of men of several aesthetic persuasions who, whatever their differences, could be counted upon to do their best, then stand aside, and far enough away, to grasp the unifying advantage of perspective.

Continuing a trend that began in the mid-twenties and would soon be decisively reversed, the *Normandie* catered to almost as many passengers in First Class as in Tourist and Third combined. Unabashedly *grand luxe*, she was so laid out as to reserve nearly all of her splendors for the affluent. Half of her clientele would be confined to lower decks. There she offered the efficient and simple accommodations presaging a time when all differences in cabins would be minor or, in some instances, nonexistent.

Boarding the *Normandie*, the privileged passenger would enter a bright reception hall—with flooring of the high gloss linoleum then common to places of public assembly—that might cheer him with its assuring air of business at sea. This was signified by the chief purser's office, an information bureau, branches of familiar Parisian boutiques, and a doctor's office with a notice stating the doctor's hours. At this point, most passengers

would want only to have a look at their cabins, to which attendant stewards were ready to escort them, and be on hand to welcome bon-voyage parties of indeterminate numbers and questionable sobriety. Others, however, would be so possessed by curiosity and the need to know precisely what would house and keep them for a special week of their lives that they would start upon ramblings open to all the serendipity of the misguided tour.

Among these, First Class passengers would not, as a rule, be counted. Conspicuous interest on their part would be considered unseemly or gauche, and liable to single them out as novices. The more likely wanderers would be passengers assigned to other classes—perhaps a man up from Tourist and alert to a rule of the sea stating that before a liner casts off, barriers between one part of the ship and another must be removed.

Beginning in the Lower Hall, this intruder might feel imprisoned between the tall medallioned doors of the dining room and the chapel's great lacquered panel of cast iron blocking his way forward. But only for a moment. The panel with its stately Norman knight in full panoply was a removable screen which, rolled to one side, would

210

Overture.

Normandie's theater—the first such amenity built into a liner—was the forwardmost of a series of grand spaces that flowed, uninterrupted, along the entire length of the ship's principal social deck. It was approached from the elevator lobby *(right)* through low railings designed by Raymond Subes, a master at wrought iron whose reputation, and spectacular work on both the *Paris* and the *Ile de France*, led naturally to his *Normandie* assignment. Subes also designed the gold-scallop-shell-punctuated fretwork of the elevator enclosures adjacent to the theater entrance.

(Below) Leading aft from the theater and elevator lobby, a long Gallerie-Salon led to *Normandie*'s Grand Salon.

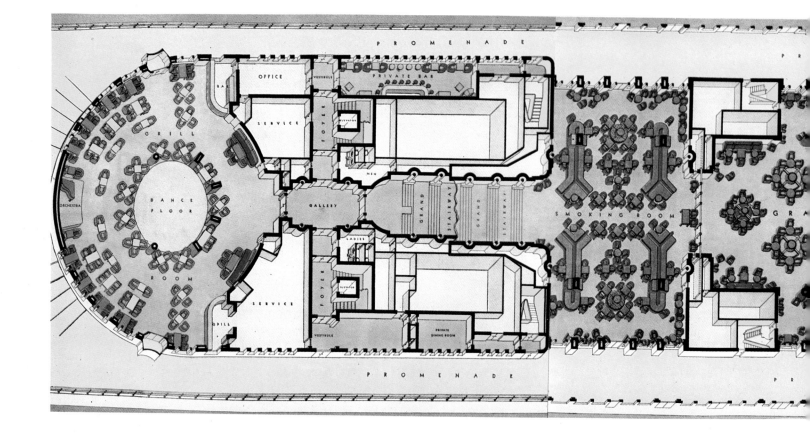

Beaux-Art-Deco.
Nineteenth-century classicism and the crossing currents of new ideas in the twentieth submit to a marriage of convenience in the *Normandie*. The result? Astonishing. When all is said and done, *Normandie* stands apart as the finest example of fully evolved marine Art Deco ever devised. Yet, as this composite plan of the ship's major public rooms demonstrates, many elements of École des Beaux Arts planning—formality, balance, ceremonial progression, the all-important *grande descente*—were evident in the designs of the ship's principal architects, Roger-Henri Expert and Richard Bouwens de Boijen. The utilitarian philosophy and engineering-based aesthetic of the International Style is not evident here (except to a minor extent in the Café-Grill at far left). But if indeed form follows function, then no more perfect harmony could exist than that between the opulent architectural setting this plan represents and the expectations of 848 First Class passengers involved in that five-day ritual of pleasure that was once an Atlantic crossing on the *Normandie*.

reveal the familiar shape and all the liturgical appurtenances of a miniature *église*. Genuflecting if he were Roman Catholic or, if not, observing the curiously contingent nature of those objects in the place that gave it an ecumenical character, he might note that the shipboard distance between Catholicism and Protestanism was but a matter of substitutions and replacements, including shutters designed to obscure, at moments, what would be offensive to either confession of faith.

What he might not be aware of was that he had entered a place of worship as aesthetically avant-garde as anything else that would appear under French auspices until Matisse's chapel of Ste.-Marie du Rosaire in Vence and Le Corbusier's Nôtre Dame du Haut in Ronchamp. Serene, yet far from sober, the seagoing chapel was distinguished first by the engraved wooden sculptures of Gaston Le Bourgeois presenting the Stations of the Cross as semiabstractions, and then by bas-reliefs of an equally simple linearity by Jan and Joël Martel, whose versions of episodes in Christian myth were carried over even to the chasubles worn by priests in the conduct of services.

Perhaps edified, but not inclined to linger, our independent explorer might take the few steps down to the swimming pool directly beneath the chapel. Entering by way of a niche-in-the-wall bar, he would be thrust into a "very temple of abstraction," meaning little more than that the *Normandie*'s pool was the conventional sound-box of clinically shiny surfaces, indirectly illuminated from overhead troughs and girded by a frieze of Sèvres stoneware tiles showing, in this case, stylized scenes of life in a bestiary. But the most unusual thing to be noted

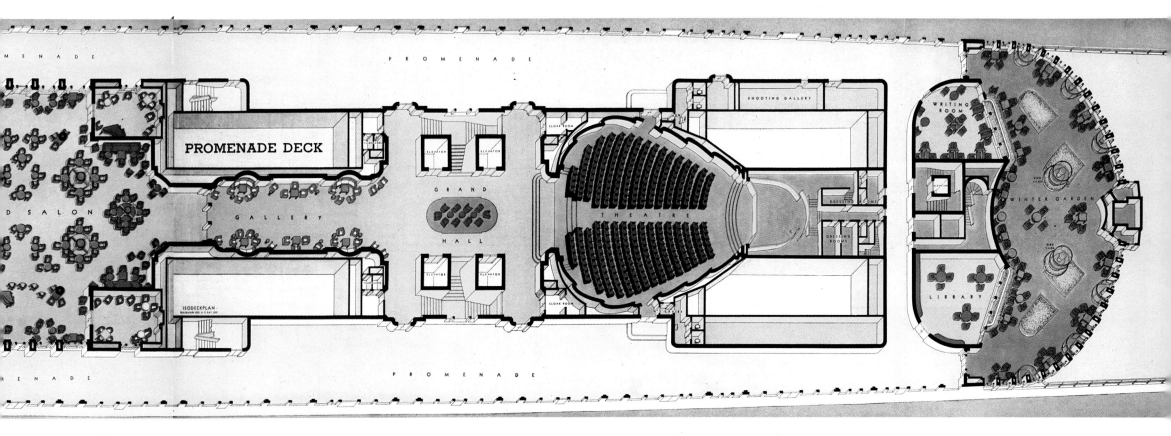

was the installation of obtrusively ugly lipstick-shaped rubber posts marking the graduated levels of the pool and serving as pillars of safety or, in rough weather, as bumpers for swimmers who, welling up with the movement of the ship, might be in hazard of being spilled into either end.

Up the stairs he had minutes before descended, our wanderer, finding the dining room doors wide open, might be moved to stand still and draw breath. His first glance would have taken in nearly three hundred feet of space in a vista four decks high. Longer than the Hall of Mirrors at Versailles, the Salle à Manger, thanks to Thomas Alva Edison, was illuminated far more brilliantly and dramatically: thirty-eight sconces, each providing almost sixteen feet of vertical light, were mere background for the twelve luminescent standards of Lalique that gave the room the appearance of a vast cave of stalagmites. Capacious enough to seat seven hundred people at one time, it was the only space on the ship to be air-conditioned. It was, in fact, the largest room on the ocean with this new convenience—something that sea travelers of a later generation would regard as incomprehensible.

Of all of the *Normandie*'s social rooms and interior esplanades, the dining room was the one most clearly conceived under the advantage of divided funnel uptakes. A rectangular playing field of light, its radiant reach was defined by a single piece of statuary—a female figure called *La Paix*—and otherwise unbroken by pillar or post. Its lavishness of space was so profligate as to allow for an entrance staircase the whole height of one normal deck and designed to serve no other purpose than as a stage from which to mount the rituals of the mealtime *grande descente*.

213

Soirée.
Le Grand Salon—an afternoon tearoom, a
cocktail hour rendezvous, a ballroom, and
a nightclub—was versatile and, like all
other social centers of the *Normandie*, so
flooded, fountained, and haloed with ar-
tificial light as to make glimpses of
daylight seem like intrusions. A kind of
subliminal trademark of the ship, the
roseate Aubusson chairs that graced her
main lounge would eventually turn up,
good as new, on the *Liberté* of 1950, and a
section from one of Jean Dupas's extravagant etched-glass allegorical murals *(facing page)*, which formed ceiling-high
"screens" at the room's four corners, is
now installed above the bar in New York's
Metropolitan Museum restaurant.

For the most part, medallions in the room's ceremonial doors featured various ecclesiastical structures from
the towns of Normandy, including the great Gothic cathedral at Rouen. By intention or coincidence, this
provided a direct connection with what the open doors would reveal. The ground plan of the dining room was
strikingly like that of the cathedral, and its walls of glass, however opaque, furthered the similarity. Even though
it was more on the order of a patriarchal cross than a Latin one, this plan was cruciform, with a nave running
from the entrance to a choir, one deck below, that fanned out in a semicircle enclosing the Banquet Room. This
adjunct to the restaurant—one of nine such private dining rooms—was of modest capacity, and dominated by a
bas-relief celebrating—much in the manner of art work on the *Bremen*—the bare-breasted fecundity of Norman
womanhood and the husbandry of its winemakers, herdsmen, and fisherfolk. (One of the more memorable uses
of the privacy of the Banquet Room was a dinner on June 21, 1939. On that evening, Fred Snite, a man whose
affliction had made him a celebrity—with only his head sticking out of a torpedo-shaped iron lung—was rolled
into place at a long table in order that he might play host to a private party.)

Still taking in the dining room's vista of napery, Daum crystal, and Christofle silver, our newly embarked

Paradis des Fumeurs.
(Following pages) Obviating the need to
find means of conveying to women passengers that they were indeed welcome in
the decidedly masculine ambience of *Normandie*'s Smoking Room, Expert and
Bouwens deftly arranged that the question
should never arise since—en route from
Grand Salon to Café-Grill—members of
both sexes would, perforce, pass through
the center of the Salon de Fumoir. Page
216 shows details of Albert Dunand's
sculpted and lacquered allegorical panels
from the firewall dividing Grand Salon
from Smoking Room. Page 217 shows the
Smoking Room decorated by Dunand in
the same technique with scenes of hunting
and fishing in a manner "reminiscent of
the Egyptian." *(Panels on p. 216 courtesy of
Bruce Newman, Newel Art Galleries, New
York City)*

naif might then be impelled to take a flight of stairs to the Upper Hall, there to find himself between the closed
draperies of the theater—the first auditorium of its kind ever installed on an ocean liner—and the closed doors
of the Grand Salon, two contiguous galleries away. So poised, he might then defer the pleasures of either, step
onto the enclosed Promenade Deck, and make an end run around to the Winter Garden forward. There, great
plate-glass windows looking onto the waves ahead would, once the ship was at sea, glint with sealight meant to
give a natural look to budgerigars and other birds in tall aviaries surrounded by displays of flora carefully

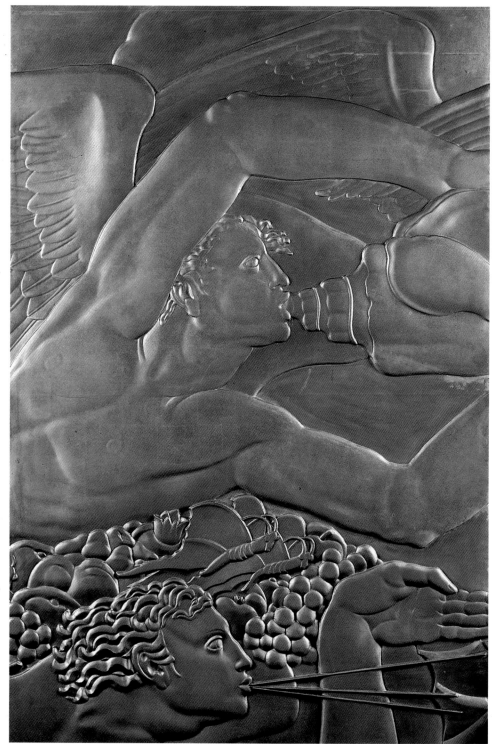

Last Resort.
With an orchestra, a dance floor, and until 1936 a panoramic view over the stern *(facing page)*, the Café-Grill was an informal getaway from *Normandie* protocol. By day an alternative setting for luncheon for anyone in the First Class, by night an à la carte restaurant for those seeking exclusivity, the stern-most public room on *Normandie*'s Promenade Deck forfeited its privileged view—but not its cachet—in the ship's second season, when French Line directors decided to add a Tourist Class lounge behind it and, in so doing, eliminated one of the Atlantic's most extraordinary amenities.

selected to represent all regions of France. The persistence of wicker, however strangely the stuff was shaped into tub-like chairs and parson's tables, was inescapable. Behind the Jardin d'Hiver, and looking through windows placed so as to look onto it, were the Writing Room, of enough quietude to encourage the best of postcard prose, and the Reading Room, all but empty of books, that seemed more like a trysting place than a *bibliothéque*.

Around to the Upper Hall once more, our observer would be in a position to experience the full Beaux Arts *ampleur* and ceremonial splendor that made the *Normandie* a reassertion of the past and not, as time has confirmed, a preview of the ships of the future. Should the few intervening fire walls be open, his view from the theater steps would encompass the tunnel formed by the Upper Hall and Grand Gallery, through the Grand Salon and across the Smoking Room to the broad steps leading up to the Café-Grill—a distance of nearly seven hundred feet, longer than two football fields, that continued beyond the line of sight to the windows of a semicircular terrace overlooking the ship's wake.

Steady of purpose, he might then press on to find that the Grand Salon combined a roseate aura of Aubusson with the gleaming gold and silver of murals by Jean Dupas. These panels of etched glass screened four corners of the room with a bold, almost undulating illusion of movement. Translucent fantasies, they presented new versions of Greek myths and united these with a recurrent motif of waterborne craft recapitulating maritime enterprise from the days of triremes to those of the high-funneled paddle-wheelers of the early nineteenth century.

Two and a half decks high, with a verticality emphasized by tall paired columns, fountain-like shafts of light, and two enormous high-standing vases of pewter, the Grand Salon somehow remained cozily inviting. Circular settees of the sort found in Victorian hotel lobbies and long wall-side *canapés* added conviviality to chairs conversationally grouped about little circular tables. The overall effect was to make this most severely formal of all spaces on the ship unexpectedly informal.

Passing through the Salon into the Smoking Room, our impostor would come to one of the most extraordinary volumes of ship space ever devised—a social hall with the atmosphere of a grand concourse widened, cross-beam, before the sweep of it continued up the five landings of a broad staircase turned into "transparent architecture" by colonnettes of light under the presiding grace of a larger-than-life-size statue (the very same one that today stands, all but hidden and unrecognized, in the gardens of Miami Beach's Fontainebleau Hotel).

The master of ceremony, so to speak, who gave the walls of the Smoking Room a kind of paleological sobriety edged with touches of witty irreverence was Jean Dunand. His four sculptured bas-relief panels, each twenty feet square, demonstrated just about everything that ingenious mixes of lacquer and bonded companies of males could do in the pursuit of Fishing, Horse Taming, Harvesting, and Sports. Technically, Dunand handled these subjects with a sculptural precision and a virtuosity with lacquer that made particular use of his own invention of a bold white—produced from eggshells crushed into powder and mixed with resins—applied first to the bikinis of ancient athletes and then to the squares of checkerboard tables. This tour of the masculine world of picturesque employment, macho domination of mild beasts, pastoral lassitude, and decathlon competition was saved from documentary banality by a playfulness of approach toward historical manifestations of folk art in general and, in particular, its famous Egyptian and Japanese renderings.

Up the broad stairs aft and between their palisades of light, our investigator would then come to a room different from anything he had seen since crossing the gangplank. In the congeries of the *Normandie*'s modes and styles the Café-Grill posed the possibility, or confirmed the truth, that "less is more." Not yet the cliché it would become in the lingo of design, the phrase made reference to the startling economy of glass, chrome, and polished marble as presented by Ludwig Mies van der Rohe at the Barcelona Pavilion of 1929 and which—along with the tables and chairs that became instant classics bearing his name—took modernism into probably its most elegant phase.

A handsome anachronism in its Beaux Arts setting, the Café-Grill, designed by Marc Simon, had walls of varnished pigskin, tables and chairs of stainless steel, a ceiling lighted by languid arabesques of glass and supported by square-cut pillars of black marble. As if it were an afterthought occurring just before the possibilities of the *Normandie* were about to run out, the Grill nevertheless found its place in maritime history as the most successful expression of modernism on the Atlantic—excepting, perhaps, only the "black bar" on the *Michelangelo*, of which it was the promise and first incarnation.

Conspicuous Privacy.
Normandie offered two *appartements de grand luxe*, called "Deauville" and "Trouville," which were without equal on the Atlantic run. Each consisted of a living room, dining room with service pantry, four bedrooms, and the option of two additional rooms for servants. Located aft on the Sun Deck directly above the Café-Grill, these palatial suites took full advantage of their position with curved walls, large windows, and broad, crescent-shaped private decks from which the privileged occupants *(right)* could, from a decent remove, survey the activities of other passengers on the terraced after-decks.

Having gone as far as he could go in the First Class "avenue within the pod of the hull," our Tourist Class visitor then had two choices. He could conclude his tour and descend to his own part of the ship or, still unsated, ascend to the Sun Deck and hope that a friendly room steward might allow him to peek into the suites designated *de grand luxe*.

The prime apartments were the Deauville and the Trouville—each with three double bedrooms and one single, three baths, a lounge, dining room, service pantry, and a "promenade terrace" overlooking the stern. Like two other such suites, they came with grand pianos and individualized schemes of decor. These ranged from the shiny-surfaced *moderne*, as in the Rouen Suite, to the reproduction, as in the Jumièges Suite, of the eighteenth-century chambers where the Marquise de Pompadour spent the last years of her life in the Château de Bellevue. This extraordinary range of styles, extending even to "ordinary" First Class accommodations, included the few

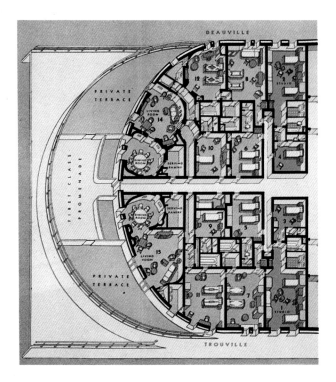

Deauville.

Like those on *Queen Mary*, the *Normandie*'s de luxe suites were equipped with the adjustable fresh air ducts and indirect lighting which, like the bouquet of a wine or the radiator cap of an automobile, tell with precision the years of their respective appearances.

The most admired of *Normandie*'s two six-room *suites de grand luxe*, the Deauville *(right)* was notable for the delicacy of its color scheme—including a blond ash grand piano—and the mixture of airiness and gravity that conjoined the new trend toward simplicity with a preference, characteristically French, for the substantial. *(Deauville Suite courtesy of Peter Boyd-Smith)*

Comings and Goings.
(Right) The salon of the Rouen Suite. With walls of lacquer and pigskin, it expressed designer Dominique's commitment to the avant-garde. *(Below)* In one of only two period-style units on *Normandie*, this is the bedroom of Nelson's Jumièges Suite.

high-tech all-metal staterooms of a dirigible sparseness designed by Madames Blanche Klotz and Lucie Renaudot.

All in all, it was this mélange of preferences that gave the *Normandie* her character as a kind of aesthetic entrepôt and perhaps justified the intentions of those in charge of her who "wanted to reconcile history with modernity and repair the linkage of the ages."

Our wanderer, having seen how the other one-tenth of one percent of the population lives at sea, might finally be ready to go below and introduce himself to his bunkmates in the closet-sized cabin where they would share a single porthole and a bathroom down the hall. Five decks above, the strains of "La Marseillaise" from the Pont Promenade would tell him that the greatest ship in history, casting off, was on her way.

AFTERWORD

Our themes have been two: the ocean liner as a showcase for representative period decor and the ocean liner as a reflection of the social ethos for which it is itself a metaphor. Together they define "the transatlantic style."

Perhaps the clearest example is the way by which, in the sorriest years of the Great Depression, sea travel entered a kind of minor golden age predicated less on elitism than on freedom of choice. Behind this development were two factors having more in common than was originally apparent. The first was a change in the makeup of life at sea in which the security of an old social order was undermined by the self-conscious glamour of a new one. When celebrity and notoriety became of more account than eminence or aristocracy, "society" quietly closed its doors, reaffirmed its own discriminations, and, like the "huddled masses" of a previous generation, disappeared forever from the decks of ocean liners. The second was the delayed introduction of rudimentary creature comforts, the absence of which an overemphasis on luxury had long obscured. At last, most First Class cabins had private toilet facilities, not merely Louis Quinze commodes. At last, electricity was of a wattage sufficient to read by, even in staterooms. On afterdecks, passengers no longer had to share a place in the sun with derricks, winches, and coils of greasy hawsers. Advances in refrigeration had finally eliminated the universal, century-old "ship's smell" that persisted as late as the first voyages of the *Queen Mary*. In a few lounges and dining rooms, there was even air-conditioning. All of this narrowed the gap in amenity between classes and increased the degree of respect with which segregated passengers on the same ship were treated. Travelers in Tourist and Second sailed in circumstances often superior to those of First Class twenty years earlier.

Depression-born fantasies (the production numbers of Busby Berkeley, the futuristic sketches of Hugh Ferriss) gave the thirties a glitter that was not gold; and Madison Avenue joined Hollywood to give them a character from which the Depression was tactfully omitted. In terms of sea travel, what allows those years to be called golden, rather than gold-plated, is the simple fact that—even before the arrival of the three superliners of the century—choices open to prospective passengers were of a range and variety never to be repeated.

Crowding the docks of West Side Manhattan, sometimes twelve abreast, ocean liners presented a movable feast to reporters and photographers. As, one by one, ships became the grandest, biggest, fastest, those who covered the waterfront gave sea travel its mystique. Maiden voyages brought out scores of power boats, excursion steamers, blimps, barges, and tough little fireboats spouting plumes of spray. Celebrities aboard brought press boats from which reporters clambered up rope ladders to interview Gertrude Ederle, Gertrude Stein, Gertrude Lawrence, and Gertrude Vanderbilt Whitney. To notions of high life, each disembarkation contributed its mite: Daimlers and Duesenbergs being lowered on ropes; borzois, released from their upper-deck kennels, straining at the leash; archbishops in gaiters; prizefighters with their dukes up. Movie sirens and lady tennis champions posed by railings in their cowls of fur. Polo players and best-selling authors, in chesterfields or "doggy" tweeds, smiled for cameras on sunny Sports Decks; comedians poked their heads through life preservers. In the madcap spirit of Carole Lombard in *The Princess Comes Across*, it was all fun with a wink, as desperate in its gaiety as the treasure hunts that sent the debutantes of Detroit and St. Louis in their spaghetti straps and satin shoes giggling through the slums. When, as never before, the wonders of the steamship era needed no other attention but what they legitimately called to themselves, it was the funny and the phony, inextricably fused, that increased their fame and, by the same token, diminished their grandeur with reams of paid-by-the-line "hot" copy.

"Wonderful nonsense," one historian called it, and its bread-and-circus aspects no doubt filled a need for the comforts of self-deception. If it was obvious that the dignity of privilege had been replaced by its exploitation, so had the world of affairs been reduced to gossip and anecdote by journalists and the off-guard embarrassments of the "candid" by photographers.

All the same, Marlene Dietrich, a svelte "spectacle in white," *did* one evening descend the grand staircase of the *Ile de France* and, in the hush of the moment, reach the table where Ernest Hemingway—an impostor from Second Class in a borrowed tuxedo—was quick to pull out a chair and so set in motion the still lively legend of Papa and "the Kraut."

World War II, effectively ending the luxury liner as legend, returned it to the realm of the ordinary. When Europe was once more within civilian reach, Americans indulged a long-pent hunger to discover what had survived, what was lost, what the Old World under new auspices might look like. The result was a run of prosperous years on the Atlantic without precedent.

And why not? If veteran travelers had to accept the loss of the *Normandie, Bremen, Conte di Savoia*, and nearly all of the high-funneled marvels of the twenties and thirties, they still could resume annual crossings on some of the greatest ships ever built. New travelers, hardly aware of what they were missing, could choose among the *Mary* and *Elizabeth*, the refurbished *Ile de France*, the rehabilitated *Europa* (rechristened *Liberté*), the war-aborted *Nieuw Amsterdam* and *America*, even the still-afloat remnants of Mussolini's "Italia"—*Saturnia, Vulcania, Conte Biancamano*.

But, except for a few crusty sticklers for protocol, sea travelers were no longer in thrall to that "frieze of simulated order" maintained by the captain's table, and the purser's delvings into the fine print of *Who's Who* to decide who might sit there. What most post-War travelers wanted was a reasonably swift, pleasant, and inexpensive way to get to Europe. If this meant settling for the efficiency and aesthetic nullity of a Route 66 motel or a downtown Statler-Hilton, so what?

For a while, the older ships did their best to honor past custom and to keep up the side; and their stewards and stewardesses coped bravely with a lack of demand for services they were meticulously trained to give—either because the nature of these services was unknown to the passenger or, just as often, unwanted.

Encouraged by rising profits and their promise of a never-ending demand for round-trip bookings, new ships from Holland, Italy, and the United States replaced the trappings of grandeur past with bland but serviceable pavilions of pleasure open to short-term trippers of all classes, including those cheerfully content with a berth in one of the four-in-a-box cabins of Tourist or Third. In supplying these newcomers with superb twentieth-century plumbing and round-the-clock entertainment, the steamship companies introduced features that would have struck First Class passengers of 1912 not as civilized advances but as ablutionary license and unsanctioned claims on shipboard privacy.

Once more, changes in society had called the tune, revised the standard, and given the customer what, in the bliss of ignorance, he wanted.

230

Index

Page numbers in italics indicate material in illustrations or legends.

232